Emily Post on Entertaining

Also in this series

Emily Post on Weddings

Emily Post on Etiquette

EMILY POST

on

Entertaining

Elizabeth L. Post

HARPER & ROW, PUBLISHERS   NEW YORK
Grand Rapids, Philadelphia, St. Louis, San Francisco
London, Singapore, Sydney, Tokyo, Toronto

FIRST EDITION

Designed by Kim Llewellyn

Library of Congress Cataloging-in-Publication Data

Post, Elizabeth L.
  Emily Post on entertaining.

  Includes index.
  1. Entertaining.   I. Post, Emily, 1873–1960.
II. Title.
BJ2021.P67   1987   395'.3   86-22930
ISBN 0-06-274006-7 (pbk.)

92 OPM 10 9 8 7 6 5 4 3 2 1

Contents

Introduction ix

Party Planning 1

Invitations & Replies 9

Dinner Parties 33

Table & Place Settings 43

Serving at Dinner 57

Buffets, Luncheons & Cocktail Parties 73

Other Entertaining Occasions 89

Obligations of Guests and Hosts 97

Entertaining for Business 107

Index 117

Introduction

To entertain, as defined in a dictionary, is "to show hospitality to." All the fine china and delicate crystal in the world can't equal the special qualities of graciousness, warmth and genuine hospitality given by a host and hostess to their guests.

The etiquette of entertaining begins with a code of behavior, based on kindness and consideration, and continues with the guidelines that enable you to be self-confident and comfortable in any social situation, whether it be a picnic on the beach or a formal ball. When you know you are using the right fork at a dinner party, you can relax and enjoy the party more. When you know how to word an invitation to tea correctly, you know you're starting the party well, before it even begins. And when you know whether or not to invite the boss to lunch, you're presenting an image that can only serve to help your professional life.

This book, containing all of the most-asked questions about entertaining, answers each with the guidelines that enhance your ability to be not only a wonderful host or hostess, but a wonderful guest as well.

Naturally, I hope you will find this to be informative and entertaining reading from cover to cover, but since time is a precious commodity and most etiquette questions need a quick answer, it has been arranged into specific categories to help you find the information you need at a glance. Whether your question is how to address the butler at a formal dinner or how to fold napkins for a luncheon, you will find the answers in the sections that deal specifically with these topics.

Most of this book is meant to be used as a guide, not as hard and fast rules written in granite! By taking the suggestions that apply to you, by eliminating the details that would be difficult for you or seem unnatural to you and by combining the elements that are suitable to your home and your friends, you can custom-tailor this information to fit your needs. What's most important is that you use these tools to help yourself be confident and relaxed. In this way you can give—and receive—the hospitality that makes a social situation pleasant, comfortable, gracious and graceful, as well as fun and entertaining!

Party Planning

Q. *What are the requirements for a successful dinner party?*

A. There are six requisites that contribute to a successful party.

> First, the guests should be congenial—a table full of people with nothing in common can make for strained silences or awkward conversation.
>
> A menu that is well planned and suited to your guests' tastes is another factor.
>
> An attractive table creates a welcoming ambience —with everything in perfect condition: linen pressed, silver polished, glassware sparkling.
>
> A fourth requisite is food that is well prepared.
>
> Fifth, and very important, are a gracious hostess and/or host who are welcoming and at the same time enjoy their guests. A hostess who spends the better part of the evening in the kitchen or running back and forth arranging things creates tension and cannot give her guests the attention that she should.
>
> The last factor is that any servants be competent and pleasant.

Q. *What are the considerations in deciding whether or not to have help when giving a dinner party?*

A. The key consideration is the size of your party. Twelve is the maximum number that can be served smoothly at a sit-down dinner without help. If you enjoy cooking, you know it is no problem to prepare the food for as many guests as you like, but it really isn't possible to serve more than twelve quickly and efficiently, all by yourself. For a seated dinner of more than sixteen the services of two people are recommended. Greater numbers, of course, require more help.

Q. *How do I know whether to tip temporary help?*
A. Ask when you call to make the arrangements. The method of payment varies in different localities and also depends on the policy of the agency. Some agencies send a bill for their services and prefer that you not add a tip, while others indicate on the bill that you may add a tip. Other agencies bill you their service charge but ask that you pay the help directly, in which case you would include a tip with your payment, if you wish.

If you have hired temporary help personally and not through an agency, you simply pay them before they leave at the rate you have agreed upon, including a tip if you found their work more than satisfactory.

Whatever the system, it is most important that you establish the method and amount of payment at the time you make the arrangements to avoid any unpleasantness or embarrassment.

Q. *What guidelines can you offer for selecting guests?*
A. Your primary requisite is to invite guests who are likely to be interesting to one another. It's a little like making a gift list where you try to choose presents the recipient will appreciate, not what you like. When seating your guests, remember their likes and dislikes

—avoid seating two people next to one another who are on opposite sides of a controversial issue. Should they argue, their controversy can be embarrassing and spoil the evening for other guests.

Q. *Can you offer any suggestions for choosing the menu for a dinner party?*
A. First, one should always try to choose a well-balanced meal; an especially rich dish is balanced by a simple one, never served with another rich dish. Second, consider the appearance of the food you serve so that every food is not white—creamed soup, breast of chicken, cauliflower and mashed potatoes, for example, or green—spinach soufflé, asparagus and lettuce salad. Third, combine flavors well so that every dish is not sweet nor every one spicy.

You should never serve more than six courses—even at the most formal dinner. These courses are:

1. Soup or fresh fruit cup or melon or shellfish
2. Fish course (only if shellfish is not served as a first course)
3. The entrée, or main course (usually meat or fowl, and vegetables)
4. Salad
5. Dessert
6. Coffee

Q. *What considerations affect the selection of wine?*
A. The two most important considerations are that the wine complements the food with which it is served, and that it pleases the palates of the people

drinking it. A high price does not necessarily indicate a superior wine, although it often does.

If you are unsure as to what wine to select, ask the advice of the manager of a wine shop, who is used to these questions and usually has good suggestions, and/or check your cookbooks—often wine suggestions are listed with menu ideas.

Q. *What wine goes with which dinner course?*

A. Sherry is usually the first wine offered at a dinner, generally with a soup that contains sherry.

A dry white wine is served with fish or with an entrée to which it is complementary.

Red wine is normally served with red meats, duck and game. At less formal dinners, a claret or light red wine may be drunk throughout the meal.

When champagne is the only wine served, it is served as soon as the first course has begun, and then throughout the meal. When other wines are included, champagne is served with the meat course.

Q. *Which type of wineglass is used for what wines?*

A. Sherry, which is served at room temperature, is poured into small, V-shaped glasses.

White wine, which is served well chilled, is poured into round-bowled, stemmed glasses.

Red wine, which is served at room temperature, is poured into less rounded, more tulip-shaped glasses that are narrower at the rim than are white wine glasses.

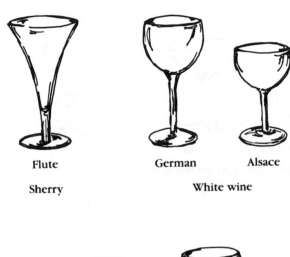

Flute   German   Alsace

Sherry   White wine

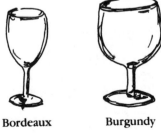

Bordeaux   Burgundy

Red wine

Types of wine glasses

Champagne, which is served very well chilled, is poured into either flat, wide-rimmed glasses or into champagne flutes (stemmed glasses that are long and narrow).

Two types of champagne glasses

Invitations
& Replies

Q. *How is an invitation worded for . . .*
. . . a formal dinner?
A. An engraved invitation to a formal, private dinner reads:

> *Mr. and Mrs. James Sebring*
> *request the pleasure of your company*
> *at dinner*
> *on Saturday, the twelfth of June*
> *at half past seven o'clock*
> *253 East Delaware Place*
> *Chicago, Illinois 60611*

R.s.v.p.

It is also appropriate to use a fill-in, engraved invitation, where a portion of the invitation is already printed and the specific information is added by hand:

> *Mr. and Mrs. Anthony Pierce*
> *request the pleasure of*
> *Mr. and Mrs. Baldwin Vance's*
> *company at dinner*
> *on Saturday, the second of October*
> *at eight o'clock*
> *3 Fox Run*
> *Concord, New Hampshire 03301*

R.s.v.p.

If the dinner is held in honor of someone, "to meet Mr. Quentin Maltby" may be written by hand at the top of the invitation.

When the invitation is handwritten rather than engraved in full or in part, the wording is the same as either of these examples.

Q. . . . *a private dance?*

A. The form used most often is:

> *Mr. and Mrs. Alexander Gifford*
> *request the pleasure of*
> *Miss Alyce Korn's*
> *company at a dance*
> *Friday, the first of June*
> *at ten o'clock*
> *Manursing Island Club*
> *Rye, New York*

R.s.v.p.
10 Stuyvesant Avenue
Rye, New York 10580

Another appropriate form is:

Mr. and Mrs. Stephen Bellows
Miss Marissa Bellows
request the pleasure of your company
on Friday, the eighth of September
at ten o'clock
22 Old Oaks Drive
Dallas, Texas 75201

R.s.v.p.   *Dancing*

Q. . . . *a charity benefit?*
A. These invitations are accompanied by a card stating the amount of the subscription, the address to which it should be sent, etc. Often the committee or the patrons of the event are printed inside the folded invitation.

The Governors of the Metropolitan Opera Club
invite you to subscribe to
A Midwinter's Night Ball
to be held at
The Union League Club
on Saturday, the seventeenth of January
nineteen hundred and eighty-seven
at
half past nine o'clock
New York, New York

R.s.v.p.

Q. . . . *a public ball?*
A. The word "ball" is rarely used except in an invitation to a public or semipublic one—such as may be given by a committee for a charity or association of some sort. For a private dance, the word "dance" is used rather than "ball."

The Junior Section of the Women's Club of Boulder
requests the pleasure of your company
at a Ball
to be held at Greenhaven Country Club
on the evening of Thursday, the twenty-third of March
at ten o'clock
for the benefit of
The Youth Counseling Service
single ticket: $25.00   *Black Tie*
couple: $45.00

Q. . . . *a reception or a tea?*
A. A formal invitation to a reception or a tea includes either the phrase "At Home" or "will be at home" or ". . . at Home." The time is not set at a certain hour; rather, the beginning and terminating hours are indicated.

An invitation to a tea would read as follows.

Mrs. Louis Gelbach
Miss Susan Gelbach
will be at home
Wednesday, the ninth of November
from five until seven o'clock
340 Park Avenue

An invitation to a reception to meet a distinguished guest has the guest's name engraved at the top:

To meet the Honorable Reginald Peabody
Mr. and Mrs. David Hill
at Home
Thursday, the fifth of September
from eight until ten o'clock
237 East 17th Street

Q. . . . *an affair with more than one host?*
A. The name of the person at whose house the party will be held is usually placed first on the invitation. Or, if one is a great deal older than another or than the others, his or her name may head the list. The invitation should make clear where the event is to take place and where the acceptances and regrets are to be sent. If a dinner is to take place at a club or a restaurant, for example, the form is as follows.

Mr. and Mrs. Charles Henry Bates
Mr. and Mrs. George David MacLellan
Mr. and Mrs. John Scott Blackman
request the pleasure of your company
at dinner
Friday, the sixth of February
at half after seven o'clock
at
The Shore Club
R.s.v.p.
Mr. and Mrs. Charles Henry Bates
103 Midland Avenue
Oak Park, Illinois 60303

If a luncheon is to be at Mrs. Bates's house instead, the correct form is this:

Mrs. Charles Henry Bates
Mrs. George David MacLellan
Mrs. John Scott Blackman
request the pleasure of your company
at a luncheon
Wednesday, the eleventh of February
at half after one o'clock
103 Midland Avenue
Oak Park, Illinois 60303
R.s.v.p.
Mrs. Charles Henry Bates

Q. *What sort of written invitations should I select for a formal dinner party?*

A. Invitations to very formal dinners may be engraved or written by hand in the third-person style. Less formally, they are written on notepaper or an informal note. For most less formal occasions the attractive, decorated, preprinted invitations available at stationers and card stores are perfectly acceptable and practical.

Q. *What does a third-person formal invitation look like?*

A. A formal invitation is engraved or thermographed on white or cream cards, either plain or plate marked, or it is handwritten on personal notepaper.

The typeface is a matter of personal choice. The store where you order your invitations will have samples to show you.

Punctuation is used only when words requiring separation occur on the same line, and in such abbreviations as "R.s.v.p." The time is never given as nine-thirty, but as half after nine o'clock or half past nine o'clock.

If the event is to be given at one address and the hostess lives at another, her address should appear below the R.s.v.p., assuming that she wishes replies to go to her home.

If the party is formal, the phrase "black tie" or "white tie" appears in the lower right-hand corner of the invitation.

Q. *Are titles used on formal invitations?*

A. Yes, always. The title "Miss" is not used on formal wedding invitations before the bride's name, but is used on all other formal invitations.

Q. *How do handwritten formal invitations differ from engraved invitations?*

A. They vary little. The wording and spacing must follow exactly as they would if the invitation were engraved. The cream or white paper used may be plain or it may include a very small monogram, but it may never be headed by an address. If the family has a crest or coat of arms, it may be stamped, without color, on the invitation.

Q. *Is it acceptable to use informals as invitations?*

A. Yes, if the card is engraved with your name, the invitation is written this way:

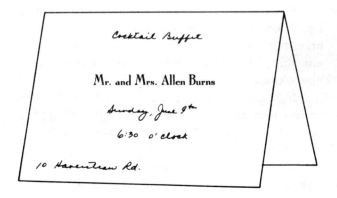

If the card is monogrammed or plain, the invitation takes the form of a brief note and must include your name. It is correct, if you prefer, to put "Regrets only," in the lower left corner, followed by your telephone number or address—instead of the more formal "R.s.v.p."

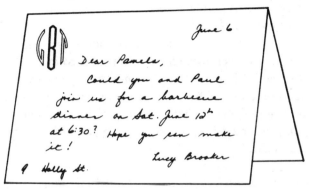

June 6

Dear Pamela,

Could you and Paul join us for a barbecue dinner on Sat. June 13th at 6:30? Hope you can make it!

Lucy Brooker

9 Holly St.

Q. *How far in advance of a party should invitations be issued?*
A. Between two and three weeks ahead of time, and they should be answered at once.

Q. *We received an invitation on a commercial, fill-in card worded in the third person. Do we reply as if it were a formal invitation?*
A. No, even though the wording is third-person, this is not a formal invitation and need not be answered as such. A brief note or a telephone call (if the number appears on the invitation), or your own informal with "So sorry, must regret the 17th," or "Looking forward to the 17th with pleasure," is all that is necessary.

Q. *Is it ever acceptable to extend an invitation by phone?*

A. Yes. Telephone invitations are correct for all but the most formal dinners.

Q. *If a cocktail party is held before a dinner dance or other function may a guest accept the invitation to one event but not the other?*

A. No, unless the hostess specifically says, "Please join us first even though you can't come to the dance afterward." In most cases, it is not up to you to make this suggestion. The only exception would be with very close friends where you might say, "I'd love to join you for a drink, but we are going to dinner at the Hartmans."

Q. *Do the invitations to a cocktail buffet differ from invitations to either a cocktail party or a buffet?*

A. Yes, in that invitations to cocktail parties alone usually state the time as "cocktails from 5:00 to 7:00," whereas invitations to a cocktail buffet or a buffet state only the time the party begins.

Q. *What do BYOB and BYOF mean on an invitation?*

A. "BYOB" means "bring your own bottle." The bottles are not intended as gifts for the hostess and host but are to be used by the guest for his or her cocktail and then may be taken home again. The host and/or hostess provide mixers and soft drinks.

"BYOF" means "bring your own food." It rarely

appears on invitations in that form. Rather, the terms "potluck" or "chip-in dinner" are used.

Q. *What are reminder cards? When are they used?*
A. When invitations have been telephoned, extended verbally or sent out several weeks in advance, a reminder card may be sent on an informal or on notepaper. You simply write: "To remind you—Wednesday 10th, 7:30."

If you are expecting houseguests but have not confirmed the arrangements you might write:

Dear Helen,
    Just to remind you that we are expecting you on the fifteenth. Can't wait to see you!

        Love,
        Lisa

Q. *What are answer cards?*
A. They are the least preferable form of obtaining a reply to an invitation, but they are acceptable. They are usually small cards that are engraved in the same style as the invitations they accompany. Answer cards have a place for the invited guest to check whether he or she will attend or not. It is not a good idea to have a fill-in space for "number that will attend" since some recipients assume this means they may bring additional guests.

Answer cards with invitations to private parties often include a self-addressed, stamped envelope.

When you return an answer card, you do not also send a formal reply.

Q. *When an invitation has to be recalled, what form is used? Is the reason for the recall of the invitation given?*

A. If time is very short, a cancellation may be hand-written or given by telephone. If there is time to have a card printed, either of the following forms is correct. Generally, a reason is given, unless it is the cancellation of a wedding after the invitations have been issued:

> *Owing to the illness of their daughter*
> *Mr. and Mrs. Carl Junggren Peterson*
> *are obliged to recall their invitations*
> *for Tuesday, the tenth of June*

or

> *Mr. and Mrs. Aaron Shapiro*
> *announce that the marriage of their daughter*
> *Susan*
> *to*
> *Mr. Norman Green*
> *will not take place*

The invitations are not actually returned by the invited guests—in this case the term "recall" is another way to say postponed or canceled.

Q. *Is it permissible to ask a hostess to extend an invitation to someone?*

A. No. When regretting an invitation because you have guests yourself, you should explain your reason to the hostess. She then has the option to say, "I'm sorry you can't come—we'll miss you!" or, if she is having a buffet or a cocktail party where one or two unexpected guests won't make a difference in her planning, she may say, "Do bring them. I'd love to meet them."

Q. *Is it okay for one member of a couple to accept an invitation and the other to decline? How would the response be worded?*
A. Yes, it is proper to take for granted that one alone will be as welcome as both. The acceptance is worded as follows:

> *Mrs. Andrew Cernek*
> *accepts with pleasure*
> *Mr. and Mrs. Henk's*
> *kind invitation for*
> *Saturday, the fifth of July*
> *at eight o'clock*
> *but regrets that*
> *Mr. Cernek*
> *will be unable to attend*

Q. *How soon after receiving an invitation should I reply?*
A. As soon as you possibly can.

Q. *How is a formal reply worded?*

A. The general rule is "reply in kind." Once learned, the formal reply is the easiest to write, because it is written in the same form as the invitation, substituting the order of names. The reply should be written in the third-person form if that is the style of the invitation. In accepting the invitation you must repeat the day and hour so that any mistake can be rectified. But if you decline an invitation it is not necessary to repeat the hour.

If the invitation reads:

> *Mr. and Mrs. Richard Deane Barth*
> *request the pleasure of your company*
> *at dinner*
> *on Saturday, the ninth of September*
> *at half past seven o'clock*
> *630 Duer Road*
> *Sebastopol, California 95472*

R.s.v.p.

the acceptance reply would read:

> *Mr. and Mrs. Samuel Leader*
> *accept with pleasure*
> *the kind invitation of*
> *Mr. and Mrs. Richard Deane Barth*
> *for dinner*
> *on Saturday, the ninth of September*
> *at half past seven o'clock*

Another option, which is not quite so formal, is:

Mr. and Mrs. Samuel Leader
accept with pleasure
Mr. and Mrs. Barth's
kind invitation for dinner
on Saturday, the ninth of September
at half past seven o'clock

The formula for regretting the invitation reads:

Mr. and Mrs. Samuel Leader
regret that they are unable to accept
the kind invitation of
Mr. and Mrs. Richard Deane Barth
for Saturday, the ninth of September

Or, equally acceptable:

Mr. and Mrs. Samuel Leader
regret that they are unable to accept
Mr. and Mrs. Barth's
kind invitation for dinner
on Saturday, the ninth of September

Q. *To whom is the reply to a formal third-person invitation addressed?*
A. Your reply is always addressed to the person or people from whom it was received. If it is from "Mr. and Mrs. Oscar Felcher" your reply is sent to Mr. and Mrs. Oscar Felcher. If it is from two or more hosts or

hostesses, your reply is sent to the one at whose house the party is to take place, or if it is to be at a club or hotel, etc., to the name and address indicated below the R.s.v.p. If there is no indication, you must address your reply to the first name or to all the names listed on the invitation in care of the hotel or club.

Q. *How does one know where to send a reply?*
A. One sends a reply either to the address shown under the R.s.v.p. or the address that is included in the body of the invitation. In the event that an answer card is enclosed, its envelope is often the only place the address is shown.

Q. *I received an invitation with R.s.v.p. followed by a telephone number. May I still respond through the mail?*
A. Yes. If for some reason you are unable to reach the host or hostess by telephone or if the telephone call is long distance and you would prefer not to incur a telephone charge, you may reply by mail, as long as you do so immediately.

Q. *What does "regrets only" mean?*
A. It means that you reply only if you are unable to attend the function. Do not reply if you plan to attend.

Q. *May informals be used for replies?*
A. Yes, so long as the invitation is semiformal or informal. If you are able to attend you might write, "We're looking forward to the 18th at seven o'clock!" or, if you cannot attend, "So sorry, must regret the 18th."

Q. *We received an invitation to a public charity ball but are unable to attend. Must we respond, and if so, how?*

A. No, one does not need to refuse this type of invitation. The return of the filled-in response card and the check for the tickets constitute an acceptance but regrets are not expected.

Q. *When more than one person hosts a dinner how is the reply worded?*

A. When you write your answer you repeat all the names that appear on the invitation, even though the envelope is addressed only to the name following the R.s.v.p., or to the first name on the list of hostesses.

Mr. and Mrs. Darius Cook
accept with pleasure
the kind invitation of
Mr. and Mrs. Goldsmith and
Mr. and Mrs. Crawford and
Mr. and Mrs. Peyton
for Tuesday, the third of June
at half after seven o'clock

If you must regret the invitation, you would write as follows.

Mr. and Mrs. Darius Cook
regret that they are unable to accept
the kind invitation of
Mr. and Mrs. Goldsmith and
Mr. and Mrs. Crawford and
Mr. and Mrs. Peyton
for Tuesday, the third of June

Q. *I don't drink alcoholic beverages. Must I decline cocktail party invitations?*
A. No. Every good hostess has soft drinks of some kind available, or club soda or mixers. Many people do not drink alcoholic beverages and there is nothing wrong with saying, "No, thank you" to an alcoholic drink and asking for a soda instead. If you are concerned that there will be nothing suitable for you to drink, take a bottle of something you like. Leave it in the car unless, upon your arrival, you find there is literally nothing you can drink at the party, in which case excuse yourself for a moment and bring in your bottle.

If you morally disapprove of drinking in general, you should refuse the invitation, but do so without expressing your disapproval.

Q. *Must I give a reason when I refuse an invitation?*
A. No, you need not give a reason. The general "reply-in-kind" rule holds. In fact, if you are declining simply because you don't want to go or dislike the host

or hostess but have no other plans, it is best not to give a reason, if asked, other than "I'm terribly sorry, we're busy that evening." This leaves you free to accept another invitation. If you make up an excuse, such as an out-of-town trip, you may not then accept another invitation without risking hurting the feelings of those who invited you first.

If you genuinely are unable to accept an invitation from a good friend and feel a formal, third-person reply is too unfriendly, you may write a personal note explaining your refusal.

Q. *What type of social events require a "pay-back" invitation?*
A. Parties in private homes, whether luncheons, brunches, cocktail or dinner parties, do require a return invitation. Wedding and shower invitations, invitations to dances or balls and invitations to any official function or one that you pay to attend carry no "return" obligations.

Q. *If I refuse an invitation am I obligated to return the invitation?*
A. Yes, although it is a milder obligation than if you had accepted the host's hospitality. His or her intent to entertain you was there and should be acknowledged by an invitation from you in the not-too-distant future.

Q. *We've extended an invitation to return a dinner party invitation but our hosts refused. I feel obligated,*

but don't want to make a pest of myself. Should we extend another invitation?
A. Yes. One attempt to return the invitation after a dinner party is not enough. You should try at least once, and preferably twice, more.

Q. *What are the valid reasons to change an acceptance to a regret?*
A. The only acceptable reasons are illness, death in the family or a sudden, unavoidable trip.

Q. *How do I change my response to an invitation: from no to yes? from yes to no?*
A. If the party to which you were originally invited is a large reception, a cocktail buffet, a picnic or any gathering at which one or two more guests would not cause a complication, you may call the hostess, explain that circumstances changed and ask if you may change your regret to an acceptance. If, however, the party involves a limited number of guests, such as a seated dinner, a theater party or bridge, the hostess will surely have filled your place and it would embarrass her if you asked to be reinstated.

To change your response from yes to no, it is important that you call immediately, explain your problem and express your regrets. If there is ample time, you may write, if you prefer, giving the reason and your apologies. In any event, it is essential that you let your hostess know right away.

Q. *If I decline a dinner invitation for a certain evening, am I free to accept another dinner invitation for the same evening?*

A. Yes. You may not, however, accept one dinner invitation and then cancel when you receive an invitation you would prefer to accept to dine elsewhere.

Q. *An unexpected business trip forced one of my guests to cancel her acceptance two days before my dinner party. Would it have been proper to ask a friend to fill in?*

A. Yes. A close friend may be asked and should be flattered you feel you can count on him or her, not insulted that he or she was not included in the first place.

Q. *Should I mention my diet to my hostess when accepting her invitation?*

A. If you are the only guest invited, you may and should mention your diet to the hostess since she will be preparing a meal just for you. If the invitation is to a dinner that will include several guests, however, don't mention that you are on a weight-loss diet or that you are a vegetarian when you accept the invitation because she will feel obligated to change her menu or prepare something special for you. You may tell her privately when you arrive, saying, "I am a vegetarian and I just wanted to tell you so you'll know why I'm not eating the meat." Or you may take a very little meat but just leave it on your plate. If you are concerned that you won't then have enough to eat, have a snack at home before the dinner party.

If you follow dietary restrictions because of health or religious reasons, it might be better to discuss it with your hostess beforehand, telling her you will bring a dish for yourself, prepared according to your restrictions. If the dinner is a formal "public" one, you might have to refuse the invitation.

Q. *What does it mean when an invitation specifies a certain type of dress? Just what do "white tie," "black tie," "formal" and "semiformal" mean?*

A. "White tie" is the most formal evening wear— white tie, wing collar and tailcoat. This is almost never required today, except for official and diplomatic occasions and a rare private ball. For a woman, "white tie" indicates a long gown should be worn.

"Black tie" or "formal" is a tuxedo with a soft shirt and bow tie. Jackets may be white in the summer and black the rest of the year, or are available in patterns and many other colors. Women usually wear long dresses, but a short or cocktail-length dress is acceptable.

"Semiformal" means women wear dresses or good slacks and men wear sports shirts and slacks. Neither should wear T-shirts or jeans. In some areas, "semiformal" means dresses for women and suits and ties for men. If in doubt, it is perfectly acceptable for you to check with your hostess.

Dinner Parties

Q. *What is a formal dinner?*
A. Almost any dinner where guests are seated at a table and are served by someone other than themselves is considered a "formal" dinner today. Naturally, there are several degrees of formality, from large, "official" formal dinners to small, at-home dinners.

Q. *Are guests ever announced at a private dinner party?*
A. Never. The only time dinner guests are announced is at large, official functions when the hostess or host may not know all those who have been invited.

Q. *How long should I plan for cocktails before serving dinner?*
A. Dinner should be planned for at least an hour later than the time on the invitation, but no longer than ninety minutes.

Q. *If guests do not move toward the dining room after dinner is announced, what can a hostess do?*
A. She may ask two or three good friends to lead the way, or she may approach one conversational group and insist that they start moving toward the dining room.

Q. *Should guests bring their cocktails to the dinner table or finish them before entering the dining room?*
A. They should carry their cocktails with them only if the hostess suggests that they do so. If a guest asks, "May I take my drink?" the hostess cannot refuse, but

she can discourage others from doing so by simply not offering the suggestion.

Q. *Does the host and/or hostess lead the way into dinner?*
A. Only at a very formal dinner. Then the host leads the way with the woman guest of honor, whom he seats on his right. The hostess is always the last to go into the dining room at a formal dinner unless a male President of the United States or a male governor in his own state is present. In these exceptional cases the hostess would go in to dinner with the guest of honor. They would lead the way and the wife of the President or governor would follow immediately with the host. Other guests walk in with whomever they are talking to when dinner is announced.

Q. *If there are no place cards, how do guests know where to seat themselves?*
A. The hostess tells them where she would like them to sit.

Q. *When place cards are used, do guests sit down as soon as they find their seats or wait until the hostess enters?*
A. Women sit down as soon as they find their places, even though the hostess remains standing ur.til everyone is at his or her chair. Men do not sit down until the hostess is seated.

Q. *When place cards are used, how are they labeled: first and last name or courtesy title and last name?*

A. The courtesy title and surname—"Dr. Coleman," "Mr. Wolf"—are used at official dinners except when there is more than one guest with the same surname, in which case "Mr. Ansel Wolf" and "Mr. William Wolf" are written to make the distinction. At a dinner party of friends and/or relatives, first names are used.

Q. *Do men hold the chair for women on their left or on their right?*
A. Men hold chairs for the women on their right. The male guest of honor, even though he has escorted the hostess in, seats the lady on his right and the man on the hostess's left seats her.

Q. *Where do the host and hostess sit at a dinner party for . . .*

     . . . six, ten or fourteen guests?
A. Since this seating works out evenly, the hostess sits at one end of the table (usually the end nearest the kitchen) with the host sitting opposite her and the men and women alternating on either side.

Q. *. . . eight, twelve or sixteen guests?*
A. To avoid seating two women and two men together, the hostess moves one place to the left so that the man on her right sits opposite the host at the end of the table.

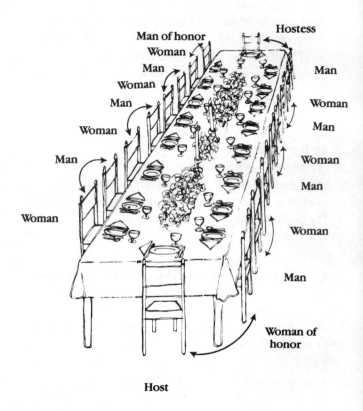

The women are seated by the men indicated by the arrows.

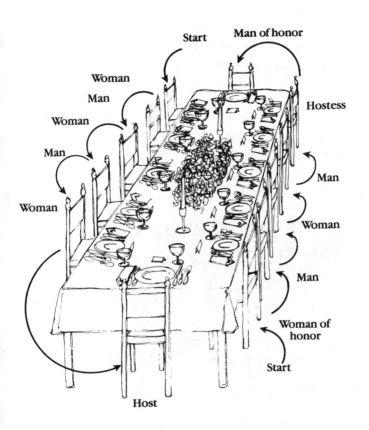

*Seating arrangement for a party of eight, twelve or sixteen.
Arrows indicate order of service.*

Q. *Where are the guests seated at a dinner with a hostess but no host?*

A. Usually a hostess will ask a friend to act as host. He therefore would sit at the head of the table, the traditional seat for the host, and guests' seating would be arranged with men and women alternating on either side.

Other options are to seat the woman guest of honor at the end of the table opposite the hostess, or simply to alternate men and women around the table

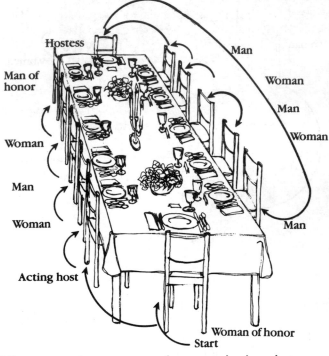

Hostess

Man

Man of honor

Woman

Man

Woman

Woman

Man

Woman

Acting host

Man

Woman of honor
Start

The correct seating arrangement for a group that has a hostess but no host. Arrows indicate order of service.

with the traditional host's chair being taken by who-
ever ends up there as part of your seating plan.

Q. *How are the host and hostess seated when there is
more than one table?*
A. The host should sit at one table and the hostess at
another. A good friend may be asked to act as surro-
gate host at another table and see that wine is served
or plates refilled.

Q. *Are husbands and wives seated together at a dinner
party?*
A. No, they are usually separated. Since they have
the opportunity to talk together all the time, having a
different dinner partner offers the chance for comfortable conversation with people other than their own
spouses.

Q. *What is a dinner envelope? How is it used?*
A. Dinner envelopes are rarely used anymore, except
at very formal official dinners. A dinner envelope has
a man's name on the outside and inside is a card with
the name of the woman he is to escort to the table and
sit beside. When used, they are organized in rows on
a silver tray and put in the front hall. The tray is
presented to each man before he joins the other
guests, just after his arrival.

Another option is a foldover card with the man's
name on the outside and his partner's name on the
inside. Below her name is a small diagram showing the
table, the location of the door and their seats. If there
are several tables, the table number is included.

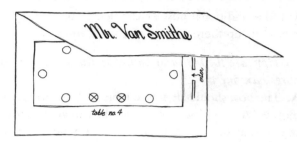

Q. *Where are honored guests seated at a dinner party?*
A. The woman who is guest of honor sits on the host's right and the man who is guest of honor sits on the hostess's right. The woman next in importance sits at the host's left, and her husband, or the man of next importance, on the hostess's left.

Q. *I prefer that my guests do not smoke at my dinner table. Must I announce this fact or is the absence of ashtrays on the table a sufficient hint?*
A. The absence of ashtrays on the table is an unspoken request that you prefer your guests not to smoke at the dinner table. If someone actually lights a cigarette or requests an ashtray, you may ask them to wait until after dinner when you have adjourned to another room.

Q. *What rules apply to dinner conversations?*
A. The unbreakable rule is that you must, at some time during dinner, talk to both your neighbors. Other, more flexible rules are that you do not talk at length about yourself, that you listen to your neighbor's point of view and that you not "talk shop" at great length to the exclusion of others seated near you.

Table & Place Settings

Q. *What rules govern formal table settings?*
A. There is only one rule for a formal table and that is that everything must be geometrically spaced: the centerpiece in the actual center, the places at equal distances and all utensils balanced.

Q. *May I use a lace tablecloth for a formal dinner?*
A. Yes. White damask is the most conservative tablecloth, suitable in any dining room. Embroidered or lace tablecloths are particularly appropriate for low-ceilinged, old-fashioned rooms. Do not use felt or other padding under a lace tablecloth.

Q. *How are cloth dinner napkins folded? Are they folded the same way if they contain a monogram?*
A. A truly formal damask dinner napkin matches the tablecloth and is approximately twenty-four inches square. They, and other very large napkins, are folded into a smaller square. The two sides are then folded under, making a loosely "rolled" rectangle. The napkin is not flattened down completely.

If large napkins are monogrammed at the corner, be sure they are folded so that the monogram shows at the lower left corner of the rectangle. If the initials

are at the center of one side of the napkin, be sure they are folded so that they appear in the center third of the rectangle.

Smaller napkins may be folded in the same way, making only two folds to form the smaller square, then folding the ends under to form the rectangle.

A smaller napkin may also be folded once in each direction and then folded in half diagonally with the two end points folded under, leaving the monogram showing in the center point.

Q. *Where are napkins placed: to the left of the place setting or in the center of the plate?*

A. For a formal table setting, the napkins are placed in the center of the service plate with the monogram, if any, facing the diner. They are put at the left side only when a first course is put on the table before the guests are seated.

Q. *What do place cards look like? Can I use any size card as a place card?*
A. For formal dinners, place cards should be plain white, or white with a narrow gold border. Decorated place cards are acceptable for a special holiday such as Christmas or Thanksgiving, and cards for a wedding or twenty-fifth wedding anniversary dinner may be bordered with silver. Place cards also may be monogrammed in silver or gold, or a family crest may be engraved at the top. Place cards are generally about two inches long by three quarters of an inch high after folding in half, although they do vary somewhat.

Q. *Where are the place cards placed on the table: in front of the plate or on top of the napkin?*
A. They may be put on top of and in the center of the napkin if they are balanced there. If not, they may be placed on the tablecloth above the service plate at the exact center of the place setting.

Q. *Must my silver and china always match for a dinner party?*
A. It is not necessary that all silver match, although spoons, knives and forks should match at each place setting, unless you have knives with crystal or carved-bone handles. These may be used with any pattern. Dessert silver, which is not on the table but is brought in with the dessert plates at a formal dinner, need not match the dinner forks. After-dinner coffee spoons are frequently entirely different.

China, too, may be mixed, but all the plates for

a particular course at one table should match. For example, all the service plates must be of one pattern, but the dinner plates, while matching each other, may be of an entirely different pattern. You may use silver or glass butter plates and condiment dishes, and glass salad or dessert plates may be used with any fine china.

What must match is the quality of everything put on the table. It would be incorrect, for example, to use heavy pottery salad plates with fine china dinner plates.

Q. *How many candles would be used during dinner?*
A. The number of candles used depends on whether the dining room is otherwise lighted. If candles alone light the table, there should be one candle for every person. If the candles are used in addition to other lighting, two or four candles are adequate for a table of up to eight persons.

Q. *When are the candles lit, before or after guests enter the dining room?*
A. They are lighted before the guests come to the table and remain lighted until they leave the dining room.

Q. *I'm planning a formal summer dinner at eight-thirty, but it won't really be dark until nine. May I use lighted candles on the table?*
A. Yes. Although candles should not be lighted during daylight hours, it will be approaching darkness at the time of your dinner, or your curtains will be drawn, so it is correct for you to light them.

Q. *I attended a dinner party where the hosts had placed small dishes of candied fruit and chocolate mints at the corners of the dinner table. Are they there for decoration or are the fruit and candy to be eaten?*

A. These dishes are left where they are placed through the entire meal and then are passed after dessert is finished.

Q. *Is there an ideal distance separating place settings?*

A. About two feet from plate center to plate center is ideal, particularly when chair backs are high. If the chairs have narrow and low backs, people can sit much closer together, especially at a round table. On the long, straight side of a rectangular table, there should be at least 6 inches of space between the chairs.

Q. *What does a formal place setting consist of?*

A. A formal place setting consists of:

- Service plate, positioned so the pattern "picture" faces the diner
- Butter plate, placed above the forks at the left of the place setting
- Wineglasses, positioned according to size
- Salad fork, placed directly to the left of the plate, assuming salad is served after the entrée
- Meat fork, positioned to the left of the salad fork
- Fish fork, positioned to the left of the meat fork; since it is used first, it is to the outside left
- Salad knife, just to the right of the plate

- Meat knife, placed to the right of the salad knife
- Fish knife, positioned to the right of the meat knife
- Butter knife, positioned diagonally at the top of the butter plate
- Soup spoon and/or fruit spoon placed outside the knives
- Oyster fork, if shellfish is to be served, beyond the spoons; this is the only fork ever placed on the right
- Napkin

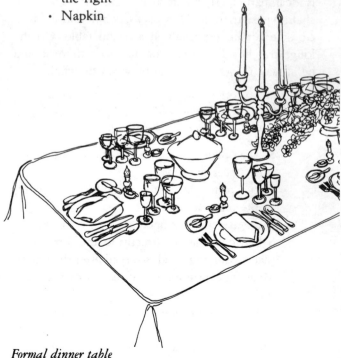

Formal dinner table

Knife blades are always placed with the cutting edge toward the plate.

No more than three of any implement are ever placed on the table (with the exception of the use of an oyster fork making four forks). If more than three courses are served before dessert, therefore, the fork for the fourth course is brought in with the course; or the salad fork and knife may be omitted in the beginning and brought in when salad is served.

Dessert spoons and forks are brought in on the dessert plate just before dessert is served.

Formal place setting

Q. *I grew up thinking butter plates weren't used during formal dinners. Is that still the rule?*
A. No, custom has changed and the use of a butter plate is now correct.

Q. *How are wineglasses arranged at a place setting?*
A. They are arranged according to size so that the smaller ones are not hidden behind the larger ones:

> The water goblet is placed directly above the knives at the right of the plate.

> The champagne glass is next to it at a slight distance to the right.

> The claret or red wine glass or white wine glass is positioned in front of and between the water goblet and champagne glass.

> The sherry glass is placed either to the right or in front of the wineglass.

Rather than grouped, wineglasses may be placed in a straight row slanting downward from the water goblet at the upper left to the sherry glass at the lower right.

Q. *My life-style is anything but formal. What rules apply to a less than formal dinner table?*
A. As at a formal dinner, everything on the table should be symmetrically and evenly spaced. Otherwise, you have much more latitude in planning an informal, casual or semiformal dinner than you do a formal dinner. You may use color in your table linens or other table appointments. Candles are used, just as

they are on formal dinner tables, but usually as single candles rather than candelabra. They may be of any color that complements your table setting, but they must be high enough so that the flame is not at the eye level of the diners.

Q. *How does an informal place setting differ from a formal one?*
A. For an informal place setting, there is less of everything. There are fewer courses served, so fewer pieces of silver are set out. The typical place setting for an informal three-course dinner includes:

- Two forks, one for dinner placed at the far left and one for dessert or salad positioned directly to the left of the plate
- Dinner plate, not on the table when guests sit down
- Salad plate, to the left of the forks
- Butter plate, placed above the forks
- Dinner knife, next to the plate on the right (for steak, chops, chicken or game birds it may be a steak knife)
- Butter knife, placed diagonally across the butter plate
- Two spoons, a dessert spoon positioned to the right of the knife and a soup spoon to the right of the dessert spoon
- Water goblet, placed above the knife
- Wineglass, positioned slightly forward of and to the right of the water goblet

- Napkin, placed between the forks and the knife

The knife blade should face to the left and, if you prefer, the dessert spoon and/or fork need not be beside the plate. Instead, they may be brought in, as at a formal dinner, with the dessert plate, or they may be placed horizontally, European style, above the center of the place setting, with bowl and tines to the left.

If you plan to serve coffee with the meal, the cup and saucer go to the right of the setting, with the coffee spoon on the table at the right of the saucer.

Service plates are not used at an informal dinner, except in an appropriate size and style under a stemmed glass used for shrimp cocktail, fruit cup, etc. and under soup plates.

The dinner plate should not be on the table when you sit down, assuming you wish it to be warm when the food is served.

Informal three-course dinner place setting

Q. *When faced with an array of flatware, I'm never sure where to begin. Which utensils do I use first?*

A. There should never be any question of which silver to use—it couldn't be easier to know! You always start with the implement of each type that is farthest from the plate.

There is one exception: if the table is set incorrectly and you realize it, you must choose the implement that is appropriate. For example, if the small shellfish fork has been placed next to the plate, you would not use the dinner fork for the shrimp cocktail and leave the little fork for the main course, even though they were placed in that order. Otherwise, you assume that the table is correctly set and you work your way toward the center with each course.

Q. *Where do I put my silver when I'm finished eating?*

A. When you have finished the main course the knife and fork are placed beside each other on the dinner plate diagonally from upper left to lower right. The handles extend slightly over the edge of the plate. The dessert spoon or fork is placed in the same position. If dessert is served in a stemmed bowl or in a small, deep bowl on another plate, the dessert spoon is put on the plate, not left in the bowl. If the bowl is shallow and wide, the spoon may be left in it, or on the plate below it, as you wish.

Q. *How does a hostess signal the end of the meal?*

A. She lays her napkin on the table and the guests then lay their napkins on the table—not before the hostess does. When the hostess rises, guests also rise and go wherever she indicates.

Serving at Dinner

Q. *In what order are the courses served at a formal dinner?*

A. The following order is customary:

> The first course is either soup, fresh fruit cup, melon or shellfish (clams, oysters, shrimp).
>
> The second course is a fish course, which is omitted if shellfish is served as a first course.
>
> The third course is the entrée, or main course, which is usually roast meat or fowl, and vegetables.
>
> The fourth course is salad.
>
> The fifth course is dessert.
>
> The sixth course is coffee, usually not served at the dining table.

Q. *Are dishes served from the left and removed from the right, or vice versa?*

A. Dishes are always presented at the left of the person being served and preferably are removed from the right. (An easy way to remember this is "RR"—remove right.) However, if it is more convenient, it is permissible to remove them from the left. The exception is that glasses are filled and additional knives are placed at the right simply because that's where they are—to present them from the left would necessitate reaching over the guest.

Q. *How does a couple serve at a dinner party without help?*

A. The most convenient solution is to have the guests serve themselves from a side table or buffet and then seat themselves at the dining table.

If you do not have facilities to do this, or prefer not to, eliminate the first course at the table. Instead, serve substantial canapés with cocktails. You may also serve cold soup, oysters, clams or smoked salmon in the living room before going into the dining room.

When the guests are seated, after you have lighted the candles, filled the water goblets and carried the food to be served to the dining room, the host carves the roast or serves the casserole and vegetables. The vegetable dishes may, however, be passed around the table instead. The host hands the hostess the filled plates to pass to the guests.

When salad is served, it is best that the guests pass the bowl, each one in turn holding it for the person on his right.

Dessert may be served already placed on individual dessert plates, or the hostess may serve it at the table as the host did the roast.

When the table is cleared by the hostess alone or with one close friend assisting, the dishes are removed two at a time, never stacked. Salt and pepper containers and condiment dishes are cleared also. To accelerate the clearing process, it is quite correct to bring back salad and salad plates, dessert plates or whatever is needed for the next course when you return from the kitchen. Or, as soon as you have removed the host's plate, you may give him the dessert to serve while you finish clearing.

Q. *At a formal dinner, how are courses presented if you have two servers? How is dinner service different if only one server helps the hostess?*

A. If there are two servers they are able to serve the first course, remove it and continue with the entrée. One fills and refills the water goblets and wineglasses. One passes the principal dishes and the second follows with the accompanying dishes or vegetables. No serving dishes or platters are ever put on the table except the ornamental compotes of fruit or candy. The meat is carved in the kitchen or pantry; vegetables, bread and condiments are passed and returned to a side table or the kitchen.

If there is only one server, the first course should be on the table when the guests sit down. The helper removes the plates when everyone is finished and either replaces each with a hot plate or places a stack of hot plates in front of the host, depending on how the main course is to be served. If the host is carving and serving at his place, the helper takes each plate and places it in front of a guest.

While the guests are eating, the helper straightens up the living room and prepares the dessert and the coffee tray.

When the guests have finished, the hostess rings and the helper clears the table and serves dessert, either already on plates or by passing it to each guest.

Q. *I've rarely been to dinner parties where the hosts have servants so I'm not sure how to treat them. Do I* *talk with them as they serve dinner? Do I make requests of the servants or of my host or hostess?*

A. No, you do not talk with them as they serve dinner, other than to say, "No, thank you" or "thank you." If you know a servant well and have not seen her or him before a small dinner, you would greet her briefly when she passes something to you, saying, "Good evening, Mary—nice to see you," or whatever you wish.

If you have a special request of which your hostess is not aware, you may ask the servant directly, so long as it's a reasonable request (a replacement for a dropped utensil, for example) and not an unreasonable order or demand.

Q. *Who is served first? Does the service then proceed clockwise or counterclockwise around the table? Who is served last?*

A. The lady of honor on the host's right is always served each dish first. The servers then move counterclockwise, serving the host last. When a single woman entertains, the lady on the acting host's right or the lady sitting at the opposite end of the table (if that is the way the seating works out) is served first.

Q. *Is the hostess ever served first?*

A. No, never, with one exception—if a very hard-to-serve dish is being presented, the hostess would be served first, explaining that she asked that this be done so she could remove the first portion, making it easier for her guests to help themselves.

Q. *Should any guest begin eating before the host or hostess is served?*

A. It is incumbent upon the host or hostess to ask guests to begin a hot course after three or four people have been served. This keeps the food of those who have been served first from getting cold. Although most of us have been raised to wait for the hostess to "lift her fork" before starting, this is true only for a first course and for dessert. For a hot entrée, if she forgets to encourage guests to begin, it is not incorrect for them to start eating after three or four have been served.

Q. *When I am offered a serving dish with a serving spoon and fork, how do I hold them?*

A. The spoon is held underneath, with the fork prongs turned down to help hold the portion on the spoon.

Q. *What is the proper way to serve champagne?*

A. From its own bottle with a napkin wrapped around it to catch drops that might otherwise fall on the guest or the table. The napkin also protects the proper chill of the bottle from the warmth of the server's hands.

Q. *Which is filled first, water or wineglass?*

A. I prefer to have the water glasses filled before the guests enter the dining room. If they are not, then the server fills the water glasses first, from the right, as soon as the guests are seated. The wine is then served, after all water glasses are filled.

Q. *When is bread served? Is it placed on the butter plate by the server or do guests help themselves?*
A. As soon as soup is served, bread is offered, passed to each guest. Each guest helps himself with his or her fingers, and places the bread, roll, crackers or whatever on his butter plate. Bread is passed again during the main course.

Q. *What is a serving table used for?*
A. It holds stacks of plates, extra forks and knives, finger bowls and dessert plates. In addition, all serving dishes, after being passed, may be left on the serving table on a warming tray in case they are needed for a second helping. If serving dishes are not left on the serving table, they may be taken to the kitchen to be kept warm until passed a second time.

Q. *Must both serving spoon and fork be supplied for all dishes served at dinner?*
A. Not necessarily. Both are supplied when needed, but if the dish is not difficult to help oneself to, a single serving spoon is more convenient. Or, instead of serving spoons and forks, there are various special lifters and tongs for certain vegetables that may be used instead.

Q. *What is a saltcellar and how is it used?*
A. A saltcellar is a tiny, open bowl used for serving salt. It usually is accompanied by a tiny silver spoon that often has a gold bowl (gold is not corroded by salt as easily as silver).

If there is no spoon in the saltcellar, use the tip of a clean knife or, if the saltcellar is for you alone, you may take a pinch with your fingers. With either the spoon or knife tip or fingers, sprinkle the salt where you need it. Salt that is to be dipped into should be put on the bread-and-butter plate or on the rim of whatever plate is before you.

Never salt your food without tasting it—it's insulting to your hostess or the chef and could spoil the taste of food that may have been amply seasoned during preparation.

Q. *At a formal dinner what is the proper way to eat . . .*

. . . chicken, game hens and frogs' legs?
A. At a formal dinner, they are not picked up in the fingers. Cut off as much meat as you can, one bite at a time, and leave the rest on the plate.

Q. *. . . clams and oysters on a half shell?*
A. They are speared with a small shellfish fork, or the smallest fork provided, dipped into the sauce and eaten in one bite. They are never cut up. They may also be eaten by taking a little of the sauce on the fork and dropping it onto the clam or by squeezing a few drops of wedged lemon juice on them.

If oyster crackers are served they may be crumpled up in the fingers and mixed into the sauce. Horseradish, too, is mixed into the sauce, or if you prefer a very "hot" taste, a drop may be put directly onto the shellfish.

Q. . . . *corn on the cob?*
A. Corn served at a formal dinner should always be cut off the cob in the kitchen and creamed or buttered. If for some reason whole cobs are served at the table you may cut the corn off yourself, or eat it neatly by picking it up. To do this, butter only half the length of two rows at a time. Hold the cob by the ends or holders, if provided, and eat the two rows. Repeat for the next rows, two at a time, until you are finished.

Q. . . . *gravy and sauces?*
A. If there is gravy or sauce left on your plate you may finish it by putting a small piece of bread on it and then eating it with your fork. You may put it in your mouth "continental" fashion, with the tines pointed down as they were when you sopped up the gravy or sauce. This is not only correct but is a compliment to the cook.

Q. . . . *lamb chops?*
A. Any kind of chop must be eaten with a knife and fork. The center is cut off the bone and cut into two or three pieces. If the chop has a frilled paper around the end, you may hold that in your left hand and cut more meat from the side of the bone. If it does not, you must do the best you can with your knife and fork.

Q. . . . *lobster?*
A. It is more likely that lobster would be served out of the shell or in a casserole rather than whole at a formal dinner, only because it can be a little messy to

eat and usually requires the wearing of a protective
bib. If, however, you are served whole steamed or
broiled lobster, the following is the neatest way it can
be eaten: to eat the meat from the claws, crack them
slowly so no juice squirts when the shell breaks. Use
a nutcracker or clam cracker in your left hand and
remove the meat from the large claw ends and from
each joint with a pick or shellfish fork held in your
right hand (if you are right-handed; vice versa if you
are left-handed).

The tail meat is pulled out of the shell in two solid
pieces—one side at a time. It is then cut into bite-sized
pieces with a knife or the side of a dinner fork, and
dipped into melted butter, if hot, or mayonnaise if
cold.

A large bowl for shell pieces and inedible parts is
usually provided to give you more room on your own
plate, and finger bowls with hot water and lemon
slices are provided as soon as you have finished eating.

Q. . . . *mussels?*
A. Mussels and occasionally clams may be served in
their shells in the broth in which they are steamed.
The mussel is removed from its shell (which may be
held in the fingers of the left hand) with a fork, dipped
into the sauce and eaten in one bite. Empty shells are
placed in a bowl or plate. The juice or broth remain-
ing in the bowl may be eaten with a spoon, or you may
put pieces of roll or French bread on the tines of your
fork and dip the fork into the broth.

Q. . . . *shrimp?*
A. There is no denying that shrimp cocktail is very difficult to eat at a formal dinner. Among family or friends at an informal dinner it is permissible to spear a large shrimp with your fork and bite off a piece. This would never do in formal company, however. If it is not too impossibly large, each shrimp should be eaten in one bite. But when shrimp are of jumbo size, you must grasp the cup firmly with one hand and cut the shrimp as neatly as possible with the edge of your fork. It is impossible to use a knife because the stemmed shrimp cup will tip over unless held with one hand.

Q. . . . *snails?*
A. Snail shells are grasped with a special, tonglike holder in the left hand (or with the fingers, if no holder is provided) and the meat is removed with pick or oyster fork. The garlic butter that remains in the dish is sopped up with small pieces of French bread and eaten with the fork.

Q. *If a service plate is used, at what point is it removed from the table?*
A. At a truly formal dinner, from the time the table is set until it is cleared for dessert, a plate should remain on the table at every place. The meal begins with a service plate in place, on top of which the first course is served. When the first course is cleared, the service plate remains until the hot plate with the entrée is served, at which time the two plates are exchanged.

If the first course is passed instead of being served on individual plates it is eaten on the service plate. An exchange plate is then necessary before the soup can be served. That is, a clean service plate is exchanged for the used one, and the soup plate then put on top of that. However, I prefer that a smaller plate be placed on the service plate for the first course.

Q. *What should be removed from the table before dessert is served?*
A. Butter and salad plates, as well as the plates used for the entrée, are removed, in addition to salts, peppers, condiment dishes and unused flat silver. Glasses and goblets are not removed at this time.

Q. *How is dessert served?*
A. There are two methods of serving dessert. One is to put the dessert fork and spoon on the dessert plate. If the dessert is served in a glass bowl, the bowl is placed on the plate before it is served. If finger bowls are used, they are brought on another plate. The other, more common way to serve dessert is to bring the finger bowl, on a small doily, as well as the fork and spoon, all on the dessert plate. The diner puts the finger bowl, on the doily, above his plate and the fork and spoon each to its proper side.

When fresh fruit is to be served it is passed after the dessert and decorative sweets, such as mints, are passed last.

Q. *When coffee is offered after dinner must it be served in the dining room?*
A. No, it may be served in the dining room, but more often is served in the living room. Filled cups may be passed on a tray with sugar and cream or empty cups may be passed to guests who hold them, on the saucer, while the server or hostess pours. A tray with sugar and cream is then passed to each guest.

Q. *What was the reason behind women and men separating for coffee after dinner? Is this still done?*
A. The reason was that it was assumed that many women objected to the smell of cigar smoke so the men would remain at the dining room table for cigars, coffee and brandy while the women followed the hostess to the living room for their coffee, liqueurs and cigarettes.

This is still done today at very formal dinners. The hostess catches the eye of one of the women guests and slowly stands up. The others also rise and the women exit to the living room while the host suggests that the male guests remain at the table. The hostess may suggest that any guests might like to go to her room and freshen up during this time. After fifteen or twenty minutes, the men rejoin the ladies and more liqueurs or highballs are offered.

Q. *When only coffee is offered after dinner may a guest ask for tea or decaffeinated coffee?*
A. No, but you may ask if the coffee *is* decaffeinated. If it is not, simply refuse the coffee rather than ask the

hostess to make a separate pot. The hostess should have both prepared, as well as tea, and should offer them, but if she doesn't and you cannot drink regular coffee, you must go without.

Q. *Is it acceptable to ask for a second helping at a dinner party?*
A. No, it is not acceptable at a formal dinner, but is permissible at an informal one. At a formal dinner second helpings are to be offered; the hostess rings for her server when she notices that guests are ready for another portion saying, "Would you please pass the meat and rice again?" If there are no helpers and the host has served the entrée from a sideboard he or the hostess will usually urge guests to pass their plates for a second helping. To do this, leave the silver on the plate, making sure it is securely positioned. Never hold your silver in your hand or put it on the tablecloth when you pass your plate.

As a courtesy when only one person takes a second helping, a considerate hostess will take a little too so that her guest will not feel self-conscious or feel that he is responsible for holding everyone up.

Q. *When attending a dinner party at which the hostess has no help, may I offer to help her clear the table?*
A. Yes, you may offer, but don't insist if she refuses your help. Most hostesses want you to relax or prefer to follow their own system of organization by themselves.

Q. *When a single person entertains, can a close friend be called on to see to the responsibilities of host or hostess for the evening?*

A. Certainly, but be fair and explain clearly what responsibilities you expect him or her to undertake.

Buffets, Luncheons & Cocktail Parties

Q. *Do invitations to a buffet differ from invitations to more formal dinners?*

A. Yes, in that they are almost never in the formal, third-person form. They may be written on informals, notepaper or commercial fill-in invitations.

Q. *How many types of buffets are there? How are they different?*

A. There are basically two types of buffets—real buffets and seated or semibuffets. At a real buffet, guests serve themselves in the dining room and carry their plates to another room, usually the living room, where they hold their plates on their laps and set their glasses on the nearest table, on a coaster.

At a seated or semibuffet, guests are seated at the dining table or at small tables in the living room, hall or library where places are already set. The guests serve themselves from the buffet and then sit at the table rather than on the couch, etc.

Q. *How are buffet tables arranged?*

A. Unless there is ample space, omit articles that are strictly ornamental. If the party is large, put the table in the center of the room so that two lines of guests may serve themselves at once. In this case, the main dish is divided into two parts and one platter or casserole placed at each end of the table. The plates are in two stacks beside them, with napkins and silver arranged next to the plates.

Dishes of vegetables, salads, bread and butter, and sauces and condiments are on each end of the table so guests need to pass down only one side.

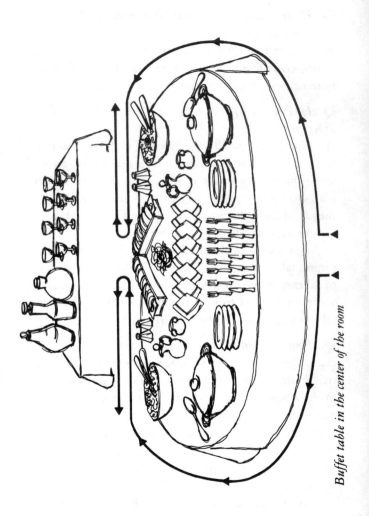

Buffet table in the center of the room

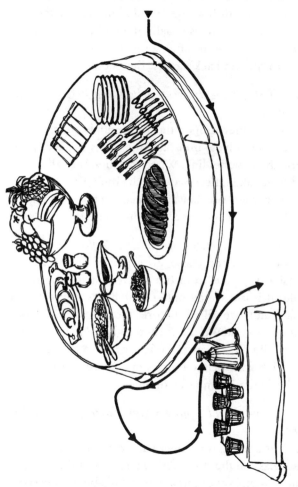

Buffet table against the wall

If the table is set against the wall, place the plates and the main dish at the end that makes for the best flow of traffic. This is usually the end nearest the entrance so that guests, after serving themselves, do not have to double back against the people coming in.

Q. *What are the duties of a host and hostess serving a buffet dinner?*
A. At a buffet dinner the host and hostess do not serve themselves until all the guests have gone through the buffet line. When the guests are all served and have taken their plates to the dining room, living room or wherever they are to eat, the host and hostess fill their own plates and join their guests.

Q. *How are beverages served at a buffet?*
A. Beverages and glasses are arranged on a sideboard or table separate from but convenient to the buffet table. If it is a seated buffet, water glasses are on the tables and are filled before the guests sit down. Wineglasses should also be at the guests' places but are never filled in advance. Coffee may also be placed on the sideboard, or the hostess may serve it from a tray in the living room after dinner.

Q. *Where should I put my glass during a buffet dinner?*
A. If there are no individual stands or tables, place your glass on the floor beside you, out of the range of others' feet. Never put a glass on a table unless coasters are provided.

Q. *How are invitations to lunch worded?*

A. Invitations may be telephoned or an engraved card may be used for an elaborate luncheon, especially for one given in honor of a noted person. Usually a formal invitation is in the form of a personal note or a "fill-in" invitation. A personal invitation might read:

> *Dear Janet and Steve,*
> *Will you come to lunch on Saturday the tenth at half past twelve to meet Nancy's fiancé, Bob Jarvis?*
> *I hope so much that you will be able to join us.*
>
>

Sincerely,
[or, Affectionately,]
Betsy (Foote)
>

If it is a very large luncheon for which an engraved card is used, "To meet Senator Murphy" is written across the top.

Q. *Are cocktails served at lunch?*

A. They may or may not be, at the discretion of the hostess. If they are, there should be juices or other nonalcoholic beverages available as well for guests who choose not to have a cocktail.

Q. *How is the table set for luncheon?*

A. Plain white table linen is not used for lunch, although colored damask is acceptable. Often placemats, or placemats plus a runner in the center of the table, are used instead of a tablecloth.

Candles may be used as ornaments, but should never be lighted in the daytime. Flowers or a decorative ornament may be used as a centerpiece, and two or four dishes of fruit or candy may be placed where they look best.

Q. *How does service at a formal luncheon differ from dinner service?*
A. The luncheon napkin is much smaller than the dinner napkin. Usually it is folded like a handkerchief, in a square of four thicknesses. The square is placed on the service plate diagonally, with the monogrammed or embroidered corner pointing down toward the near edge of the table. The upper corner may be turned under and the sides rolled loosely under, leaving a straight top edge and a pointed lower edge with the monogram still displayed in the center.

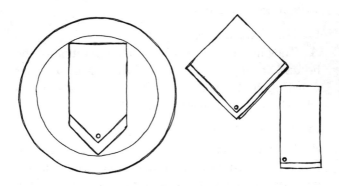

Other simple folds are perfectly acceptable also. Otherwise, formal luncheon service is identical to that for a formal dinner.

Q. *How is the service different for a less formal luncheon?*
A. For less formality, it is simpler if the first course is already on the table when guests are seated and if the main course is limited to a single dish and salad. In addition, rolls, butter and iced water and any other beverage may be placed on the table beforehand.

A buffet luncheon is another way to serve less formally. The food is set out as for a buffet dinner (see pages 75–78), but with a simpler menu. If you are having a seated buffet with a first course, it should already be on the tables when your guests arrive so they can sit down and eat it before going to the buffet table for their next course. If you have no helpers, the guests carry their empty plates and leave them on a side table as they go to the buffet table. While they are serving themselves, you may remove the used plates to the kitchen. The same procedure is followed when guests are ready for salad or dessert.

Q. *How many courses are served at a luncheon? In what order are they served?*
A. Two or three courses are sufficient at any but the most formal luncheon. There are five possible courses and you may select the two or three you wish to serve, never exceeding four courses.

1. Fruit, or soup in two-handled cups
2. Eggs or shellfish
3. Fowl, meat (not a roast) or fish
4. Salad
5. Dessert

The courses are served in the order shown above. If you choose to eliminate any courses, simply skip to the next.

Q. *What beverages are served at a lunch?*
A. In addition to ice water, wine, iced tea or coffee, hot tea and coffee or fruit punch may be served. If wine is offered, one type is sufficient, usually a light one such as a dry white wine or a claret.

Q. *When are afternoon teas given?*
A. Anytime, just to entertain your friends, or in honor of visiting friends, family, houseguests or celebrities, to welcome new neighbors, to "warm" a new house or for any other occasion that suits your fancy, from welcoming spring to perking up a dreary mid-winter day.

Q. *Are written invitations necessary for a tea?*
A. Only for a formal tea, in which case invitations may be sent on your personal notepaper or a "fill-in" invitation. Invitations to an informal tea are almost always telephoned.

Q. *How is a tea table arranged? What sort of food is served at tea?*

A. A tea table, whether the dining room table or another set up elsewhere, should always be covered with a tablecloth. Only a glass-topped table may be left uncovered. A tea cloth may be colored, but the more conventional one is of lace or white linen with needlework, lace or appliquéd designs.

A large tray is set at either end of the table, one for the tea and one for the coffee.

Cups and saucers are placed within easy reach of the women who pour, usually at the left of the tray since they are held in the left hand while the tea or coffee is poured with the right.

On either side of the table are stacks of little tea plates with small napkins folded on each one or placed in front of them.

Arranged in any way that is pretty and uncluttered are the plates of food and whatever silver is necessary. Forks should be on the table if cake with icing is served.

Food at a tea party usually consists of tea sandwiches and several kinds of sweets. Cookies, cupcakes, fruitcake or slices of iced cake are almost always offered. In addition, petit fours and miniature pastries may be served. In the winter there is sometimes a tray of hot, bite-sized appetizers, such as hot cheese puffs or pastry filled with mushrooms. Otherwise, the tea sandwiches are cold, light and delicate, such as watercress rolled in thin bread, cream cheese on date-and-nut bread or crabmeat on toast.

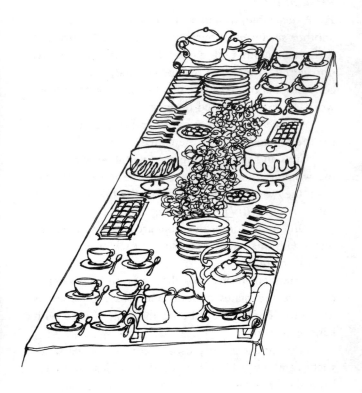

Tea table

Q. *Who "pours" at a tea, the hostess or one of her guests?*

A. The hostess asks close friends, beforehand, if they will pour and unless they have a very valid reason, they should accept. Sometimes, after an hour, the first two are relieved by two other friends.

Q. *How does a reception differ from a tea?*

A. Since receptions are almost always given in someone's honor, there is generally a receiving line, consisting of the host and/or hostess, guest of honor and, in some cases, various officials of the committee giving the reception.

The table is covered with a floor-length white tablecloth rather than the shorter tea cloth. The table is set with platters of food, small napkins (cloth or paper), plates and forks if necessary. Alcoholic drinks are served from a bar or passed, and coffee and punch are on side tables from which guests help themselves.

The type of food served differs also. Although there may be some tea-type sandwiches offered, small meatballs, dips, a cheese board, nuts, olives, etc. are added to the menu.

Q. *Are receptions ever given at home?*

A. Yes. One type that occurs quite frequently is when a groom's parents wish to give a party for their son and his bride after a wedding in her hometown to which the groom's parents' friends have not been able to travel. The reception is given to introduce their new daughter-in-law to their friends.

Q. *Are invitations to cocktail parties different from other invitations?*
A. Yes, in that they give both a beginning and an ending time, as in "cocktails from 5:00 to 7:00." Often there is no R.s.v.p. If there is an R.s.v.p., it most usually is followed by a telephone number, since this is one type of invitation that may always be answered by telephone.

Q. *What drinks are served at cocktail parties, and how much liquor is needed?*
A. All variety of alcoholic drinks are served, so it is a good idea to have scotch, bourbon, a blended whiskey, gin, vodka and rum on hand. In addition, both sweet and dry vermouth, bitters, lemons, olives, tonic and seltzer or club soda provide necessary ingredients for many drinks. Many people prefer wine to hard liquor. It is best to stock your bar according to your geographic location (for example, tequila is more popular in the Southwest than the Northeast), your own taste and the taste of your guests.

In order to best gauge quantities, keep in mind that in the winter martinis, whiskey, scotch and bourbon are the most popular drinks, while vodka, rum and gin mixed with tonic or fruit juices and white wine spritzers are more popular in the summer. As a general rule, count on each guest's having at least three drinks. A one-quart bottle will provide twenty-one 1½-ounce drinks or serve approximately seven people. In addition to the correct amount of liquor, it is important to have nonalcoholic drinks on hand, too, including tomato and fruit juices, colas, sparkling mineral waters and ginger ale or other noncola soda.

Q. *Should we hire a bartender and/or waiter for our cocktail party?*
A. It is very helpful if you plan to entertain more than eighteen or twenty people. One bartender can serve between twenty and thirty people very well. If you have a much larger party, the services of a waiter as well will help you considerably. If you have a bartender, the guests go to the bar themselves and he mixes their drinks. If you also have a waiter, he watches guests for empty glasses and offers to bring them another drink. He does this in addition to guests' going to the bar themselves.

Be sure you instruct the bartender in advance as to exactly how you like your drinks mixed and that you want him to use a measure.

Q. *What is a cocktail buffet?*
A. It is a cross between a cocktail party and a buffet dinner party where enough food is served that guests need not have dinner afterward. In addition to hors d'oeuvres, platters of cold meats and raw vegetables

or casseroles are served, buffet style, or any other offering more substantial than just hors d'oeuvres. Only one real course is served, although dessert may be offered with coffee.

Other Entertaining Occasions

Q. *How does one organize a picnic?*

A. One way is to give it yourself, inviting the guests by telephone. If they accept, tell them the hour, where to meet and whether they should bring a blanket or backrest if you don't have enough for everyone.

Another way is to call and say you are bringing the steaks, for example, and ask each person or couple to bring one dish. Ask if they'd rather bring dessert or salad, or chowder or beverages, etc.

A third way to organize a picnic is to have each family bring their own food and cook it over a community fire.

These picnics can be at the beach, a park or in the parking lot before a football game or at any other location that would be pleasant and conducive to a good time for everyone.

Q. *What are the obligations of the host and hostess entertaining friends by organizing a picnic?*

A. First, to unite a congenial group of people who won't mind some of the inconveniences a picnic often includes, whether blowing sand or ants, and who will help to make the party fun.

Second, to choose a location that is relatively insect free, and that you have visited before or have been told about on excellent recommendation. Be sure the ground is not swampy, ant-infested or covered with poison ivy. If you choose a beach, it is your responsibility to make some preparation to shield both your guests and the food from blowing sand or too much sun. It is also important to select a location that is convenient and that doesn't require that people tramp through the woods or across miles of soft sand carrying all your gear.

Third, you should plan as carefully as if you were inviting people to dine with you at home to ensure that food is served on time, prepared well and attractively presented.

Q. *Does a barbecue differ from a picnic?*
A. Only in that it is a "cooking" picnic in your own yard. Because of the proximity to your house, the menu and equipment may be more elaborate than for a picnic which must be transported in your car.

Q. *Is there a difference between a housewarming and an open house?*
A. Yes. A housewarming is specifically a party to show your new house to your friends and to celebrate your happiness at being there. It generally is a cocktail party or a cocktail buffet, as simple or as elaborate as you wish. An open house, on the other hand, is literally what the name implies. Your door is open to everyone invited between the hours stated on the invitation. It may take the place of a housewarming, but because an answer to your invitation is not expected, refreshments are simple. Dips, sandwiches, nuts and punch rather than individual drinks are good choices. Most often an open house is held to celebrate a holiday such as New Year's Day or Christmas Eve. People drop in to wish their host and friends a "Happy New Year," etc., and generally stay no longer than an hour.

Q. *What is a brunch?*

A. It is a party where a combination of breakfast and lunch foods are served, held closer to the usual hour for lunch than in the early morning. Most often brunch is informal, even casual, and while invitations may be issued ahead of time, often by telephone, it is not inappropriate to invite someone to brunch the following day. Bloody Marys, mimosas, champagne and other cocktails are often served, as well as nonalcoholic beverages, and the food is usually arranged on a buffet table, less elaborately set than for lunch or dinner.

Q. *What do you consider to be the key to a successful card party?*

A. Your careful planning of matching people who play at approximately the same level of skill and who have basically the same temperament at the same table with one another. For example, don't ever put serious players with people who chatter incessantly.

Q. *What preparations are necessary for a card party?*

A. You should be sure there are fresh cards, score pads and sharpened pencils at each table. If you have planned who will play with whom, you should place slips of paper with the names of the players who are to sit at each table on the tables or be prepared to tell each guest where he or she is to sit. You may of course prefer to have players draw for partners and then they are seated according to the suits drawn or high-low cards. It is also important to be sure that each table is properly lighted. If you are in doubt, sit at each place, hold the cards in your hand, lay a few on the table and see for yourself.

Your selection of refreshments depends on the time of day or evening your party takes place, but it should be appropriate to the time and the group. The food may be arranged on the dining room table and guests, having served themselves, return to cleared card tables or take their plates to the living room.

If it is the custom in your area to play for prizes, you must select a first prize for the highest score made by a woman and one for the highest score made by a man. At a party of women a first and second prize are usually given. The prizes should be wrapped and the recipients should open them upon receiving them.

Q. *What is the difference between a dance and a ball?*
A. Guests at a dance are approximately of one age while those at a ball can range in age from very young to very old. Also, since dances are smaller than balls, the decorations and refreshments are simpler.

Invitations to a ball are always formal and are sent out three to four weeks prior to the ball, while invitations to a dance may be written on an informal or on engraved, printed or commercial "fill-in" cards and sent only two to three weeks in advance.

The traditional dress for a man going to a ball is white tie and tails, although a tuxedo is accepted at all balls unless the invitation actually states "white tie." Men's dress for a dance can be anything from jeans and a western shirt for a square dance to a tuxedo, depending on the formality of the dance. Generally, a suit and tie is quite appropriate unless "black tie" is stated on the invitation.

Women almost always wear long dresses for a ball, but for a dance either short or long dresses are acceptable, depending on the custom of the area.

Q. *How does a man properly approach a woman to ask her to dance?*
A. If a woman is already sitting with one man, another may not ask her to dance. If she is sitting alone or in a group, he can go to her and ask, "Would you like to dance?"

Q. *If a woman refused one gentleman's invitation to dance with him may she immediately after accept a dance with another man?*
A. No. To refuse to dance with one man and then immediately dance with another is an insult to the first. In ordinary circumstances, a woman must dance with everyone who asks her.

Q. *What is cutting in and how is it done?*
A. Cutting in is when a man wants to dance with a woman who is already dancing. He steps forward, taps the shoulder of her partner (who relinquishes his place in favor of the newcomer) and begins dancing with her.

Q. *May a woman politely refuse to dance with a man who cuts in?*

A. No. She must dance with him until a third man cuts in or until the music stops. The partner who was first dancing with her should not cut back in.

Q. *Who dances with whom and in what order?*
A. At a ball, every man should dance with the hostess, the girl or girls the dance is given for if it is a debutante ball, the hostess of the dinner he went to before the dance and both women he sat beside at dinner. If he has brought a date, he must dance the first dance with her. He should also watch through the evening to make sure his date is not stuck too long with any one partner.

At an informal dance a man must dance with his hostess and dance the first and last dance with his date or wife. At a dinner dance, he dances first with the woman seated beside him.

Obligations of
Guests and Hosts

Q. *What do you consider the hallmarks of a good guest? of a good host?*

A. A good guest is enthusiastic, congenial and considerate, treating other guests and the host and hostess, as well as their property, with thoughtfulness and respect. A good host and hostess are well prepared to see to the needs of each of their guests, having carefully planned for their comfort and entertainment.

Q. *Shortly after moving to our present home we were invited to a dinner party. We arrived at 7:30 P.M., the time stated on the invitation. Not only were we the first to arrive but no other guests arrived for nearly thirty minutes. Did we do something wrong by arriving on time?*

A. No, you didn't actually do something wrong, but if the custom in your area is that guests are not expected to arrive until fifteen minutes to half an hour after the stated hour, it is wise to follow the local custom. When you entertain yourself, simply ask your guests to come a half hour earlier than you expect them to arrive. Some hostesses write, "Cocktails at 7:00, dinner at 8:30" on their invitations, which enables them to start dinner on time and allows guests leeway in their arrival time.

Q. *How long should a guest remain at a party?*

A. Dinner guests should stay at least one hour after dinner, since it is hardly complimentary to the hostess to "eat and run." At a small party a couple should not leave long before anyone else seems ready to go, because their departure is very apt to break up the party. Otherwise, a guest should stay as long as he wishes within reason, while being sensitive to noticing if the host and hostess and others at the party begin to look tired, in which case he should say his good-byes and depart.

Q. *When a party is given in someone's honor is he supposed to be the first guest to leave or the last?*
A. He is supposed to be the first to leave. This rule is more or less obsolete, however, so unless the guest of honor is the President of the United States, in which case no one may leave before he or she does, other guests may depart before the guest of honor does.

Q. *Which is better—to send flowers to your hosts before or after a party?*
A. When a party is given especially for you, you should send flowers to your hostess beforehand. Otherwise, flowers sent later as a thank-you for a very special evening are always appreciated. Ordinarily, however, neither a gift sent later nor a note is necessary. Your verbal thank-you is sufficient. A phone call the next day to say how much you enjoyed the evening is always welcome.

Q. *Should guests bring gifts of food or wine to their hosts?*
A. The custom of taking wine as a gift to a small dinner party is becoming customary. It is not too expensive or elaborate and has the advantage that if the

hostess does not want to serve it that evening because she has planned another type of wine or a different beverage, she need not do so. She certainly may offer it, but no guest should feel insulted if his hostess says, "Thanks so much! I already have wine planned for dinner, but we'll look forward to enjoying this another time!"

Gifts of food to be used for the dinner should never be taken unless the hostess has been consulted first. It is very disconcerting for a hostess who has planned a dessert to complement her meal to feel she must also serve another, unexpected dessert which may be too rich or uncomplementary. A box of candy, croissants and jam for the hosts' breakfast the next morning or another gift of food given with the statement, "This is for you to enjoy tomorrow," resolves the problem.

If it is the custom in your area to take a gift to a small dinner party, by all means do so. For a large or formal party, however, it is better not to take a gift at all, especially if you do not know the hosts well. It may not be customary among their friends, and you will only embarrass your hostess and other guests who have not brought a gift. If you do know the hosts well and you have noticed that people generally do arrive with a gift, then follow the custom of the area.

Q. *What obligations do I have toward unexpected guests?*
A. Other than the normal requirements of being courteous to any visitor, you have no actual obligation

to an unannounced visitor. If you are not busy and have no other plans, naturally you should ask him to stay. But when you are about to have a meal that can't be stretched to feed him or them, explain that you were about to eat and ask if he—or they—could stop by later. If you have enough food to include unexpected guests, of course ask them to join you. If they have already eaten, in either case, they may say so, in which case ask them to sit down with you and have something to drink.

If unexpected guests arrive when you have other social plans, say so. Your first obligation is to the people with whom you have made the plans. Tell your visitors that you are sorry but someone is expecting you for dinner (or whatever) and ask them to call you the next time they are in your neighborhood or make a definite date to get together with them soon, if you wish.

The same holds true when visitors arrive when you already have invited guests. You may ask them to join you if you are just sitting and chatting, but if you have invited a couple to play bridge, for example, your obligation is to them. Continue the game, asking the newcomers if they would like to watch. Only if the invited guests insist on stopping the game should you do so.

Q. *My husband and I are giving a dinner party without servants. Must we both greet our guests at the door?*
A. Yes, if possible. If one or the other is not available at the moment guests arrive, he or she should excuse

him- or herself and greet newcomers shortly after they enter.

Q. *How long should a hostess delay dinner for a late guest?*
A. Fifteen minutes is the established length of time. To wait more than twenty minutes, at the outside, would be showing rudeness to many for the sake of one. When the late guest finally arrives, he or she of course apologizes to the hostess and is then seated.

Q. *When a guest arrives late and we're already finished with the first course, is that course served to the late-arriving guest?*
A. No, the latecomer is served whatever course is being eaten at the time he or she arrives, unless the course is dessert, in which case he or she would be served the entrée while others have their dessert.

Q. *How do the hosts politely end a party?*
A. The first and most effective way to end a party is to close the bar. Offer "one last nightcap" and then—quite obviously—put the liquor away. The hostess may glance at her watch or hide a yawn. If these hints don't work, you can copy Peg Bracken's story about the kindly professor who said, loudly, to his wife, "Well, my dear, don't you think it's time we went to bed so these good people can go home?"

A house party hostess may perfectly properly go to bed before her guests. All she need do is say words to the effect of "If you all don't mind, I'm going to bed because the baby will be up for her bottle by six

. . . but you stay here as long as you want and help yourselves to more drinks or anything you'd like. Just turn off the lights on your way out. . . ."

Q. *If everyone is having a good time, would it be rude of the hosts to encourage their guests to remain longer?*
A. Not at all! It shows you are enjoying their company, too, and if their offer to leave seems tentative, it is far friendlier to say, "Oh, don't go—it's Friday night and we can all sleep late tomorrow morning," than to jump up and bring them their coats the minute someone says, "Well, it's getting late. . . ." If, however, they really must leave, one suggestion that they stay is enough. Don't force them to remain if they have a baby-sitter waiting or are firm in their resolve to go.

Q. *How can I discourage my guests from mixing their own drinks in my home?*
A. It is difficult to do without being insulting. You can control the situation somewhat, however, by going to the bar with the men and asking them to get out the ice or the mix or whatever while you pour the liquor yourself. You can also avoid having more than one bottle of liquor in evidence if guests seem to be heavy drinkers, and you can make it obvious that you use a jigger to pour drinks and hand the jigger to your guests before they pour themselves.

Q. *How do the hosts handle an inebriated guest?*
A. You must refuse to serve him or her more liquor. He or she may become insulting and abusive, but that

is preferable to having him or her become more intoxicated. The host then is responsible for seeing that a drunken guest is taken home by asking a good friend to take him or her, or you can go yourself if the distance isn't great, or you can call a cab, give the directions and pay for it. The person's car keys should be taken away if he or she is not willing to be taken home by someone else. If he or she has reached the point of almost passing out, two or three other guests should help him or her to a bed to sleep it off overnight. If the inebriated person has a spouse or date present, the host and hostess should offer this person accommodations, too, or see that he or she gets home safely.

Entertaining for Business

Q. *When is it permissible to extend an invitation to meet business contacts outside the office?*

A. Permissible occasions include the following:

- To thank someone for a service rendered
- To celebrate a newly closed deal
- To seek the confidence of a client or prospective client
- To share common problems
- To get to know someone better
- To ask a favor
- To propose or discuss ideas
- To introduce other people
- To simply get away from the office and relax

Q. *Whom may an employee invite to outside-the-office entertainment?*

A. You may invite a co-worker, a client, a prospective client, a peer from another company and, from time to time, any subordinates or one's secretary. You may never invite a superior to outside entertaining, however, not even to lunch at an outside restaurant, except as noted in the next question.

Q. *My husband's boss invited us to a large cocktail party at their club. Since we have neither the space nor budget for a similar affair, may we return the invitation by inviting them to a small dinner party?*

A. You are expected to return this social invitation, but his invitation need not be reciprocated in kind and a small dinner party is a perfectly appropriate way to entertain.

Q. *How does one extend an invitation to . . .*
   . . .a business lunch?
A. The invitation is extended by telephone and the date should be set at a restaurant convenient to both the host and the guest. Make a reservation, requesting a quiet table, particularly if business matters will be conducted.

Q. *. . . a business dinner?*
A. Business dinner invitations should be extended well in advance. The invitation may be extended either by telephone or by written note. It should be addressed to the business person only, at his or her office, to make it clear that spouses are not included. A reservation should be made at a restaurant convenient to both.

Q. *When an invitation includes spouses, are living-together companions included as well?*
A. Good manners dictate that a living-together partner be invited to social occasions just as a spouse is. If your partner has been excluded from an invitation because the host is not aware of your arrangement, you may ask, "May I bring Bill Adams, the man with whom I live?" The answer you receive should be, "Yes, of course." If the reply is negative, however, you must decide if you want to attend alone or decline the invitation. If you are not living with someone and are invited to a husband-and-wife business affair, you may ask, "Shall I bring a date, or would you rather I came alone?"

Naturally, office parties that do not include spouses also do not include your living-together partner or a date.

Q. *What business occasions call for entertaining with spouses?*
A. There are several occasions for which it is appropriate to entertain with spouses:

- When out-of-town business people and their spouses visit in your area
- When you return an invitation that included your spouse
- When you want to get especially close to a client
- When the occasion to which you are extending the invitation is a husband-and-wife affair, such as a formal dinner or a dance
- When you and a business associate find you have become friends and want to enjoy and share that friendship with your spouses
- When you, as boss, wish to get to know your employees personally and have them know you as a person as well

Q. *Should business associates be invited to a family wedding, or other family social occasions?*
A. Business associates should be invited to a family wedding only if it is acceptable to the bride or groom that they be there and if the wedding is quite large. If you choose to do this, be careful not to slight anyone

by failure to extend an invitation. If you invite one, invite all with whom you work, including your boss. If the wedding is smaller and more personal, however, you need invite only those business people who also are friends.

Weddings should never be used as an opportunity to pay off the business obligations of the bride's or groom's parents, or as an excuse to promote a deal or a business relationship.

Whether business people are invited to other family social occasions depends on the same considerations. If the affair is small and intimate, you need invite only business associates who are friends. If it is large and you are inviting business associates who are only that, you again should be careful not to exclude anyone who would feel left out if not included.

Q. *A client has extended a social invitation to a family gathering. I prefer to keep our relationship on a business rather than personal level. Must I accept the invitation?*

A. No, you need not accept. As with any personal invitation you wish to decline, simply extend your regrets noting that you are already busy. Keep your return invitations to the client on a business lunch or business dinner level. If the client is persistent in inviting you to more social gatherings, you may say, "Barney, I enjoy it so much when you and I get together, but my family just isn't able to include my business life into their social lives. They've asked that I not commit them to any more professional social gatherings."

Q. *How do I know whether or not to attend the funeral of a co-worker?*
A. The answer to your question depends on the type of funeral it is. You attend a private funeral only if a close friend or family member has called to ask you. A private memorial service is also by invitation only. A funeral open to the public will be so announced in the newspaper with time and place stated; anyone who wishes to attend may. When funeral or memorial services are publicly announced, all business associates, the employer of the deceased and any former associates should attend to honor the deceased and tell the family, through their presence, how highly he or she was thought of.

Q. *May business entertaining take place at home?*
A. Yes, if you wish to take the step beyond outside entertaining and make business associates feel like friends in the more relaxed atmosphere of your personal surroundings. When business associates are invited to your home, their spouses are automatically included. Occasionally a home breakfast or lunch may be held for business people alone, but this is for convenience or privacy rather than for a social purpose.

Q. *When a single woman gives a business party may she ask a male friend to act as host? What if the male friend is a co-worker? What responsibilities does this host-for-an-evening have? What responsibilities would a stand-in hostess have if a single man was giving a business party?*

A. Yes, she may ask a male friend to act as host. In fact, it eases the situation somewhat to have both a host and hostess when the business staff know each other well but where spouses may not know anyone at all. With both a host and hostess, one or the other can help make the spouses feel more comfortable.

Asking a male co-worker to help is less advisable since it places him in a relationship with the hostess, suggesting intimacy when none may exist at all.

One responsibility of a stand-in host is to handle drinks—either to serve them or to see that guests are attended to by waiters or at the bar. Another is to talk with guests, particularly the husbands of businesswomen, who may feel out of place.

A stand-in hostess helps greatly by talking with the host's business associates and helping their wives and husbands fit in.

Q. *What is the role of the spouse when business entertaining takes place at home?*
A. His or her primary role is to support you—to make your guests feel welcome, to help them enjoy being with you, as well as to assist with refreshments. In the case of a business party, there will undoubtedly be a lot of "shop talk" and it is important that your spouse be interested, that he or she ask questions and indicate the involvement of both of you in the company. He or she should also feel free to discuss his or

her profession and personal concerns, too, and to keep the conversation from being too focused on any one, specific topic for a long time. If you feel your spouse would not be able to handle this comfortably or to your (or his or her) credit, it is best to extend and return invitations outside your home where he or she will not be the focus of attention.

Q. *May an employee invite his or her boss to lunch?*
A. No, an employee should neither initiate nor return an invitation to lunch with his or her boss. The only kind of invitation from one's boss that may (and should) be returned is a social one.

Q. *Can you offer any guidelines for entertaining the boss?*
A. Although you may not invite your boss to dinner before being invited first, you are expected to return the invitation after you have been entertained. The following are a few guidelines that may make it more comfortable for you:

> Do not extend the invitation in person as you may to a co-worker. Instead, mail a written invitation.

> If you call your boss "Mr.," "Ms.," "Miss" or "Mrs." at the office, do not call him or her by his or her first name either in your invitation or as you speak during the evening, unless your boss suggests it.

> Your spouse should address your boss as you do.

If you and your spouse address your boss by title and last name, you should both address his or her spouse similarly.

It may be easier to entertain your boss if you include a few other guests. Select people with whom he or she may have common interests.

You need not reciprocate your boss's invitation in kind. For instance, you may repay a fancy dinner at a restaurant with a simple buffet dinner in your home.

Act and entertain as you normally would. Do not hire special help unless you've done so before; do not serve a hard-to-carve roast unless you can handle it; do not borrow china or glassware that you may be fearful of breaking. In other words, be yourself, and be comfortable.

Being gracious, interested and natural will impress the boss far more than outdoing yourself in a way that he or she, of all people, knows you can't afford.

Index

Acceptance of invitation:
  change to regrets, 30
  to charity benefits, 27
  after declining another,
    31
  formal, 24–25
  with more than one host,
    27
Additional guests, 22–23
Address, for reply to
    invitation, 26
Advance time for party
    invitations, 19
  to balls and dances, 94
After-dinner coffee spoons,
    47
Announcing of guests, 35
Answer cards, 21
Ashtrays, absence of, 42

Balls, 14, 94–96
  public, reply to invitation,
    27
  return obligations, 29
Barbecues, 92
Bartender, at cocktail
    party, 87
Beverages:
  for brunch, 93
  for cocktail parties, 86–
    87
  for luncheon, 82
  overindulgence by guests,
    104–5
  for receptions, 85
  service at buffet, 78
Black tie, 17, 32

Boss, entertainment by
    employee, 109, 115–17
Bracken, Peg, 103
Bread, service of, 64
Brunch, 93
Buffets, 75–78
  cocktail buffets, 87–88
  invitations to, 20
  luncheons, 81
Business associates,
    invitations to family
    events, 111–12
Business entertaining,
    109–16
Butter knives, 50
  at informal dinner, 53
Butter plates, 48, 49, 52,
    64
  at informal dinner, 53
BYOB, 29
BYOF, 29–30

Cancellation of event, 22
Candles:
  at dinner table, 48
  at informal dinners,
    52–53
  at luncheons, 80
Candy, after dessert, 49,
    69
Card parties, 93–94
Chairs, held for women at
    dinner, 37
Champagne, 6
  glasses for, 8
  placement of glasses, 52
  service of, 63

Charity benefit balls, 14
  invitations, 13
  replies to invitations, 27
Chicken, how to eat, 65
China, matching of, 47–48
Chip-in dinners, 21
Clams on half shell, how to eat, 65
Claret, 6
Clearing of table:
  before dessert, 69
  offer of help, 71
  without servants, 60
Clients, business entertaining, 112
  invitations to, 109
  with spouses, 110–11
Cocktail buffets, 87–88
  housewarming, 92
  invitations to, 20
Cocktail parties, 86–88
  before other functions, 20
  housewarming, 92
  invitations to, 20
  nondrinkers and, 28
Cocktails:
  at dinner table, 35–36
  at lunch, 79
  time allowance, 35
Coffee, 5, 59
  at buffet, 78
  after dinner, 70–71
  at informal dinner, 54
Co-host, business entertaining, 113–14

Color, in informal dinner settings, 52–53
Commercial invitations. See Printed invitations
Condiment dishes, 48
Conversation, at dinner table, 42
Corn on the cob, how to eat, 65
Couples:
  invitation accepted by one member, 23
  seating at dinner party, 41
Courses:
  for formal dinner, 5
  for luncheon, 81–82
  order of, 59
  wine with dinner, 6
Cutting in at dances, 95–96

Damask tablecloths, 45
  for luncheons, 79
Dances, 14, 94–96
  invitations to, 12–13
  return obligations, 29
Dates, for business entertaining, 111
Decaffeinated coffee, 70–71
Declining of invitation:
  formal, 24–25
  giving of reasons, 28–29
  return obligations, 29
  See also Regrets

Dessert course, 5, 59
  for luncheon, 82
  service of, 69
  serving without servants,
    60
  silver for, 47
Dessert forks, 51
  at informal dinner, 54
Dessert plates, 48
Dessert spoons, 51
  at informal dinner, 53,
    54
  position after use, 55
Diets, special, and dinner
    invitations, 31–32
Dinner dances, 96
Dinner envelope, 41
Dinner knife, at informal
    dinner, 53
Dinner parties, 3, 35–42
  announcing of guests,
    35
  delay for late guest, 103
  end of, 55–56
  gift to host, 100–101
  to honor someone, 12
  invitations, formal,
    11–12, 17
  length of stay, 99–100
  moving of guests to table,
    35, 36
  return obligations, 29–30
  service of, 59–72
  spacing of place settings,
    49
  and special diets, 31–32
  time for arrival, 99

Dinner plate, at informal
    dinner, 54
Dinners, business, 110
Dress:
  for balls, 94, 95
  for dances, 94–95
  specified in invitation, 32
Drunken guests, 104–5
Duck, wine for, 6

Eating:
  proper techniques, 65–68
  when to begin, 63
Employees:
  business invitations, 109
  invitation to boss, 115–16
End of dinner, 55–56
End of party, 103–4
Engraved invitations, 11, 17
Entertaining, ix
Entrée, 5, 59
  wine for, 6
Etiquette of entertaining,
    ix
Extra guests, inclusion of,
    22–23

Family events:
  invitations from clients,
    112
  invitations to business
    associates, 111–12
Fill-in guests, 31
Fill-in invitations, 11, 75
Finger bowls, 69
First course, plate for,
    68–69

Fish course, 5, 59
  wine for, 6
Fish forks, placement of, 49
Fish knives, placement of, 50
Flatware. *See* Silver
Flowers sent to hostess, 100
Folding of napkins, 45–46
Food:
  for brunch, 93
  for card parties, 94
  for receptions, 85
  for tea party, 83
Food gifts to hostess, 101
Food preparation for dinner party, 3
Forks, 50, 51
  for informal dinner, 53
  position after use, 55
Formal dinners, 35
  folding of napkins, 45–46
  hostess gifts, 101
  invitations, 11–12, 17
  order of courses, 59
  order of progress to table, 36
  place cards, 47
  placement of napkins, 46
  seating at, 36
  second helpings, 71
  with servants, 61–62
  table settings, 42
Formal dress, 32

Formal invitations, 17–18
  to balls, 94
  to luncheons, 79
Formal luncheons, 80–81
Formal place settings, 49–51
Formal tea, invitations, 82
Friends, as fill-in guests, 31
Frogs' legs, how to eat, 65
Fruit, after dessert, 69
Fruit course, 5, 59, 82
Fruit spoons, 50
Funerals of co-workers, 113

Game, wine for, 6
Game hens, how to eat, 65
Gifts, to hosts, 100–101
Glasses:
  at buffet, 78
  at informal dinner, 53
  for wine, 6–8
Governor of state, at formal dinners, 36
Gravy, how to eat, 65
Greeting of guests, 102–3
Guest of honor:
  departure from party, 100
  at dinner party, 12
  flowers to hostess, 100
  invitations to meet, 79
  at receptions, 15, 85
  seating of, at dinner, 37, 40, 42
  service of, at dinner, 62

Guests:
  announcing of, 35
  at card parties, 93
  at dinner parties, 3, 4–5
  greeting of, 102–3
  late for dinner, 103
  mixing of drinks, 104
  obligations of, 99
  offer of help at dinner, 71
  at picnics, 91
  unexpected, 101–2

Handwritten invitations, formal, 12, 18–19
Hard-to-serve dishes, 62
Home:
  business entertaining at, 113, 114–15
  receptions, at, 85–86
Honored guest. *See* Guest of honor
Host:
  absence of, at dinner party, 40–41
  at buffet dinner, 78
  and drunken guest, 104–5
  greeting of guests, 102–3
  more than one, invitations from, 15–16
  obligations of, 99
  seating of, at dinner party, 40–41
  single, sharing of duties, 72

Hostess:
  dancing with, 96
  at dinner party, 3
  at end of meal, 55–56
  order of dinner service, 62
  seating of, at dinner party, 37, 40
  See also Host
Hostess gifts, 100–101
Hot entrée, when to eat, 63
House parties, bed time, 103–4
Housewarming, 92

Informal dinners:
  place settings, 53–54
  second helpings, 71
  table arrangement, 52–53
Informal invitations, 17
  replies to, 19, 26
Informal luncheons, 81
Informal notepaper:
  for invitations, 18–19, 75
  for replies to invitations, 26
Invitations, 11–32
  to balls, 94
  to brunch, 93
  to buffets, 75
  for business entertaining, 109–11
  to cocktail parties, 86–88
  to dances, 94
  to luncheons, 79
  to tea, 82

Knives, 47, 50, 51
  at informal dinner, 53, 54
  position after use, 55

Lace tablecloths, 45
Lamb chops, how to eat, 65
Lighting of candles, at dinner party, 48
Linens:
  for formal dinners, 45–46
  for informal dinners, 52
  for luncheons, 79
  for reception table, 85
  for tea table, 83
Living-together companions, business invitations, 110–11
Lobster, how to eat, 65–66
Location for picnic, 91–92
Luncheons, 79–82
  business lunches, 110

Main course, 5, 59
  service at formal dinner, 61
  serving without servants, 60
Meat course, 5, 59
  for luncheon, 82
  wine for, 6
Meat forks, placement of, 49
Meat knives, placement of, 50
Memorial services, 113

Men:
  behavior at dances, 95–96
  dress, 32
  dress for balls, 94
  dress for dances, 94–95
  seating at dinner, 36, 37
Menu for dinner party, 3, 5
Monogrammed napkins, folding of, 45–46, 80
More than one table, at dinner party, 41
Mussels, how to eat, 66

Names on place cards, 36–37
Napkins:
  formal, folding of, 45–46
  at informal dinner, 54
  for luncheon, 80–81
  placement of, 46
Nondrinkers, invitations to cocktail parties, 28
Notepaper, for informal invitations, 17, 75

Obligation to return invitations, 29–30
Office parties, 111
One servant, formal dinner, 61
Open house, 92
Order of courses, 59
  luncheon, 82
Order of service, at formal dinner, 62

Oyster crackers, 65
Oyster forks, 51
  placement of, 50
Oysters on half shell, how
  to eat, 65

Pay-back invitations. *See*
  Return invitations
Payment of temporary
  help, 4
Picnics, 91–92
Place cards, 36–37, 47
Placemats, for luncheon,
  79
Place settings:
  formal, 49–51
  informal, 53–54
  matching of, 47–48
  spacing of, 49
Plates, 49, 68–69
  for informal dinner, 53
Potluck suppers, 21
Pouring, at tea, 85
Presentation of dishes at
  formal dinner, 59
  by servants, 61
President of United States:
  departure from party,
  100
  at formal dinners, 36
Printed invitations, 17
Private dances, invitations,
  12–13
Private dinner parties, 35
Private funerals, 113
Private homes, parties in,
  return obligation, 29

Prizes, at card parties, 94
Progress to table at dinner
  parties, order of, 36
Public balls:
  invitations, 14
  replies to invitations, 27

Quantities, for cocktail
  parties, 86–87

Recall of invitation, 22
Receptions, 85–86
  invitations to, 14–15
  receiving line, 85
Red wine, 6
  glasses for, 7
  placement of glasses,
  52
Regrets, formal, 24–25
  to charity benefits, 27
  to more than one host,
  27–28
Regrets only, 26
Reminder cards, 21
Removal of dishes, at
  formal dinner, 59
  without servants, 60
Replies to invitations,
  23–32
  answer cards, 21
  change of, 30
  to cocktail parties, 86
  formal, 17, 24–26
  informal, 19, 26
  with more than one host,
  27–28
  to public charity balls, 27

Return invitations, 29–30
  business entertaining,
    111, 115
  by employees, 109
R.s.v.p. *See* Replies to
    invitations

Salad course, 5, 59
  for luncheon, 82
  service without servants,
    60
Salad forks, 51
  placement of, 49
Salad knives, 51
  placement of, 49
Salad plates, 48
  at informal dinner, 53
Saltcellars, 64–65
Sauces, how to eat, 65
Seated buffets, 75
  luncheons, 81
Seated dinner parties, 35
  servants for, 3–4
Seating:
  at card parties, 93
  at dinner parties, 4–5,
    36–42
Second helpings, 71
Semibuffets. *See* Seated
    buffets
Semiformal dress, 32
Separation of sexes, after
    dinner, 70
Servants:
  at cocktail party, 87
  at dinner party, 3–4
  dinner served without, 60

Servants *(cont.)*
  tipping of, 4
  treatment by guests, 62
Service of dinner:
  courses, sequence of, 59
  order of, 62
  presentation of dishes, 59
  second helpings, 71
  by servants, 61–62
  without servants, 60
Service plates, 49, 68–69
  at informal dinner, 54
Serving table, use of, 64
Serving utensils, 64
  position of, 63
Shellfish, how to eat, 65
Shellfish course, 5, 59
  for luncheon, 82
Sherry, 6
Sherry glass, placement of,
    52
Shrimp, how to eat, 67
Silver:
  for informal dinners,
    53–54
  matching of, 47
  order of use, 55
  placement of, 50
  position after use, 55
  position for second
    helpings, 71
Single host, sharing of
    duties, 72
  business entertaining,
    113–14
Smoking at dinner table,
    42

Snails, how to eat, 67
Soup course, 5, 6, 59, 82
Soup spoon, placement of, 50
  at informal dinner, 53
Spacing of place settings, 49
Spoons:
  after-dinner coffee, 47
  formal dinner, 50
  informal dinner, 53
Spouse, and business entertaining, 111, 113, 114–15
Summer dinner party, candles at, 48
Sweets, after dessert, 69

Table arrangement:
  for buffet, 75–78
  for tea, 83
Table settings, 3
  formal dinners, 45–52
  informal dinners, 52–55
  luncheons, 79–80
Tablecloths:
  for formal dinners, 45–46
  for informal dinners, 52
  for luncheons, 79
  for reception table, 85
  for tea table, 83
Tea, instead of coffee, 70–71
Teas, afternoon, 82–85
  invitations to, 14–15
Telephone invitations, 20
  business entertaining, 110

Telephone invitations (cont.)
  to luncheons, 79
  to tea, 82
Temperature, for wine, 6–8
Thank-yous for parties, 100
Three-course dinner, place setting, 53–54
Time:
  allowance for ball and dance invitation, 94
  allowance for invitation, 19
  to arrive at parties, 99
  indication in formal invitations, 17
  to leave dinner parties, 99–100
Tipping of temporary help, 4
Titles:
  in formal invitations, 18
  on place cards, 36–37
Tuxedos, 32, 94–95
Two servants, formal dinner, 61

Unexpected guests, 101–2

Waiter, at cocktail party, 87
Water:
  filling of glasses, 63
  service at buffet, 78
Water goblet, placement of, 52
  at informal dinner, 53

Wedding invitations:
  to business associates,
    111–12
  formal, 18
  return obligations, 29
White tie, 32, 94
  invitation specification, 17
White wine, dry, 6
  placement of glass, 52
Wine:
  for dinner parties, 5–6
  as host gift, 100–101
  for luncheon, 82
  service of, 63
  service of, at buffet, 78

Wineglasses, 6–8, 49
  at informal dinner, 53
  placement of, 52
Women:
  behavior at dances,
    95–96
  business entertaining,
    113–14
  dress, 32
  dress for balls and
    dances, 95
  seating at dinner, 36, 37
Written invitations, for
    formal dinners, 17

About the Author

Elizabeth L. Post, granddaughter-in-law of the legendary Emily Post, has earned the mantle of her predecessor as America's foremost authority on eitquette. Mrs. Post has revised the classic *Etiquette* since 1965, and has written *Emily Post's Complete Book of Wedding Etiquette, Emily Post's Wedding Planner, Please, Say Please, The Complete Book of Entertaining* with co-author Anthony Staffieri, and *Emily Post Talks with Teens About Manners and Etiquette* with co-author Joan M. Coles. Mrs. Post's advice on etiquette may also be found in the monthly column she writes for *Good Housekeeping* magazine, "Etiquette for Everyday."

Mrs. Post and her husband divide their time between homes in Vermont and Florida.